Grace and Truth

George William Rutler

Grace

and

Truth

Twenty Steps to
Embracing Virtue
and Saving Civilization

EWTN PUBLISHING, INC.
Irondale, Alabama

EWTN Publishing, Inc.
5817 Old Leeds Road, Irondale, AL 35210

Distributed by Sophia Institute Press, Box 5284, Manchester, NH 03108.

Library of Congress Cataloging-in-Publication Data

Names: Rutler, George W. (George William), author.
Title: Grace and truth : twenty steps to embracing virtue and saving civilization / George William Rutler.
Description: Irondale, Alabama : EWTN Publishing, Inc., 2019. | Includes bibliographical references.
Identifiers: LCCN 2018056517 | ISBN 9781682780930 (pbk. : alk. paper)
Subjects: LCSH: Christian life—Catholic authors. | Catholic Church—Doctrines.
Classification: LCC BX2350.3 .R878 2019 | DDC 248.4/82—dc23 LC record available at https://lccn.loc.gov/2018056517

First printing

For my sister Dorothy, whose name means "Gift of God"

Contents

Preface

When it was suggested that the following television talks might be published as a book, I might have demurred if I had had to put them together myself, since transcribing the spoken word is a hard job. We do not write as we speak, nor do we speak as we write, and so I thank the editor who did the difficult work of making the spoken word coherent on paper. Originally, the following chapters were delivered only as conversations—albeit my favorite kind of conversation, in which I do all the talking.

As best I can remember, my first time on television was around 1976 on *The David Susskind Show*, which was broadcast from Manhattan. That was an early form of televised discussion, quite civilized in form and free of the self-conscious sound bites and shouting matches that have replaced intelligent conversation since then. My favorite recollection of constructive exchange was William F. Buckley's *Firing Line*. How I got involved with EWTN remains unclear even to me, but I know that Mother Angelica asked me to do some interviews, and that is how it began. Correction: Mother did not ask me; she told me. Her requests were always polite, but they also were peremptory in a way that allowed no contradiction. That was exactly thirty years ago, at a time when some ecclesiastics

were wasting millions of dollars on programming usually of a bu-
reaucratic nature, and all to no avail.

I think that Mother Angelica's personality was different from
mine, and I was surprised that we got on well. For a while, an ocean
separated us: I was doing graduate studies in England, and during
Lent of 1987 I traveled from Oxford to televise a live debate in
Birmingham (UK), and that same week I flew to do a program in
Birmingham (USA). This may have been the first time someone
was televised in the same week from two Birminghams.

Our Lord knew and knows all things, so in some way, He an-
ticipated television when He preached from a boat in Galilee to
be better seen and heard. None of His followers have had a better
opportunity to spread His Gospel than we do in our generation.
It is dreadful to think how much we squander that opportunity
and use the media so inadequately. But the effort is earnest, and
that frail attempt is offered in trust that the Living Word will look
kindly on what is inadequate.

—GWR

Part 1

Virtues and Abominations

1

The Golden Mean

or

How to Avoid Mediocrity and Embrace Virtue

*For the law was given through Moses; grace
and truth came through Jesus Christ.*

—John 1:17

Moses was the agent by which the divine pattern for existence was manifest in time and space. But the law needs grace to be lived, and it must conform to truth, without which it would dissolve into legalisms.

In the history of Christianity, few people spoke more gracefully and truthfully than John Henry Newman. In the nineteenth century, this English teacher and preacher embraced the Faith. And then, with the grace of his conversion, he explained how, throughout history, God's grace and truth had been sensed, intimated, and expressed, even by those who had not received the fullness of revelation.

Grace and Truth

Newman was a classical scholar. He had a particular fondness for the Latin writers, especially Cicero. Cicero was not only able to marshal the magnificent Latin language to express his ideas with eloquence, but he was able to convert others to his way of thinking. That is, he was not only a master of prose but a master of rhetoric. In a famous passage, Newman wrote, "Neither Livy, nor Tacitus, nor Terence, nor Seneca, nor Pliny, nor Quintilian is an adequate spokesman for the Imperial City. They write Latin. Cicero writes Roman."[1] Now, whether or not we are familiar with that cataract of Latin writers, we can understand immediately what he means: Cicero did not engage in a mere literary exercise when he conjugated and declined the words of the noble Latin language; he put his heart into it. He was able to speak heart to heart.

When Newman became a cardinal, he took as his motto a phrase of St. Francis de Sales: *Cor ad cor loquitor*, or "heart speaks to heart." These words were vivified in Newman's life. The grace and truth of Christ passed through the soul of that great man Newman to his hearers, who ceased being only an audience and became participants in the drama of salvation.

When Newman praises Cicero, when he cites those great minds of the past, he reminds us that the excellence that they represent is ours. There is no such thing as a truth about human nature and the moral life that was true once and ceased being true at another time. What is true is true forever. These great classical thinkers passed on to us their perceptions of the grace and truth that the Church would come to understand fully revealed in Christ. When these noble pagan writers had glimpses of God's grace and truth, they expressed it in terms of *virtue*.

Another hero of Newman was Horace. Like all classical writers, Horace spoke of a principal of virtue, the "golden mean," that would

---

[1] *The Idea of a University*, lecture II, section 5.

save people from one kind of excess for another. Horace probably didn't invent the term: The so-called "Seven Sages of Greece" all spoke of it one way or another. But he especially praised the man who loved, sought, and desired this golden mean: *Auream quisquis mediocritatem diligit.*

Notice that Latin word *mediocritatem*. It came into English as "mediocrity," but it didn't mean what we now mean by that word. "The golden mean," rather, was the virtuous balance between excesses. We live in a time of mediocrity—not the *mediocritas* that Horace praised, but the cowardly substitute for the golden mean that passes itself off with fine-sounding terms such as "compassion," "democracy," "fairness," and even "charity." But this is not the classical golden mean. The golden mean is not a compromise between the truth and a lie. It is the straight and narrow way between exaggerations of truth. Though the classical writers were unfamiliar with the sacramental gifts of the Holy Spirit, they knew that there is an order in this world and that virtue will guide us among the distortions of that order.

Every age has understood the dangers of mediocrity, so we cannot very well say that we are the first generation to have invented it. But we are, I think, the first culture that has made mediocrity into a virtue. We have confused mediocrity and the golden mean.

We live in a generation that seeks to be dazzled rather than enlightened, amused rather than inspired, entertained rather than challenged and converted. The golden mean, as distinct from mediocrity, chooses the good over the convenient, the true over the plausible. And therefore, heroic virtue is needed to live the golden mean well. Jesus Christ not only showed the world the golden mean; He was the golden mean. This is why He confused so many people: Some thought He was too rigid about the law while others thought He was too lax; some thought He was too worldly while others thought He was too supernatural. This balance is the content of perfection.

Grace and Truth

One way our civilization has tried to help people live the golden mean is the idea of a liberal education. We call it that because it is meant to liberate people from servility to extremes. A liberal education is meant not to inculcate partisan politics but to teach how to distinguish one's private passions from noble order.

William James, a philosopher and brother of novelist Henry, said of the liberal education that "our colleges ought to have lit up in us a lasting relish for the better kind of man [and] a loss of appetite for mediocrity."[2] He understood what the golden mean was, and he understood what a sham mediocrity was. If he leveled this criticism of colleges in his day, can you imagine what he would say now, looking at our schools and other institutions? The enshrinement of mediocrity has virtually destroyed education in Western civilization, and it has dealt a mortal blow to our system of justice and politics.

The golden mean, you see, not only defines virtue but requires virtue to be lived—virtues such as prudence, justice, temperance, and fortitude. The noble classical minds always considered virtue to be the disposition to observe the golden mean. Every virtue, in some way or another, is the golden mean between excesses. The virtue of magnificence, as the Scholastic philosophers called great generosity, is the mean between extravagance and miserliness. Holy pride—not selfish pride or egoism but the manifestation of God's dignity in the human soul—is the mean between vanity and servility. Courage is the mean between bravado and cowardliness. In the eighteenth century, Joseph Butler said that religion is the mean between credulity and infidelity—in other words, between superstition and atheism.

[2] "The Social Value of the College-Bred," address delivered to the Association of American Alumnae at Radcliffe College, November 7, 1907.

The golden mean is really the narrow gate that our Lord described: "For the gate is narrow and the way is hard, that leads to life, and those who find it are few" (Matt. 7:14). The substitute for the golden mean—cheap, servile mediocrity—is the object of God's deep scorn. In the book of the Revelation, God speaks with great severity to the Laodiceans: "So, because you are lukewarm, and neither cold nor hot, I will spew you out of my mouth" (Rev. 3:16).

Christ was crucified by mediocrities. Pontius Pilate was a paragon of mediocrity. His interpretation of the law and his administration of justice held virtue in contempt. It is no surprise, then, that when Our Lord was sent to the Cross, the mediocre Pilate made friends with the mediocre Herod Antipas. Herod wanted to be amused by Christ. He did not want to be challenged to see a larger world in the eyes of the Savior; he simply wanted someone to massage his ego. Pontius Pilate and Herod shook hands as Jesus went to the Cross, crucified by grotesque substitutes for the golden mean: human passion and human pride.

Mediocrity is not something to be passed over as an innocent defect. We need only look at the twentieth century for proof of how it has ushered into the world terrible evil. That century has written in blood for all time the consequences of excess. The classical world had its defects; the ancients knew carnage well. Many times, in their weaker moments, they participated in holocaust upon holocaust—but they never pretended that mediocrity was the same as virtue, the same as the golden mean.

The Jewish philosopher Hannah Arendt wrote a book about Adolf Eichmann, one of the chief architects of the Holocaust, called *Eichmann in Jerusalem*. He was one of the most diabolical figures ever to have walked upon the human stage. Yet, Arendt remarked, what a surprise it was, when he finally was found and put on trial, to see what an ordinary man he was in appearance and speech. In him was nothing that looked or sounded like the devil. But that is what made his evil all the more palpable! Arendt used this example to coin the expression "the banality of evil." In other words, evil loves to work through mediocrity. Evil smiles. Evil will speak with a kind of humanitarianism, all while holding virtue in contempt. It does not believe in the possibility of grace. It considers truth to be only a matter of opinion.

A mediocre civilization, as part and parcel of its rejection of the goodness of God, loses a sense of evil and, specifically, how evil came into the world. That is, it rejects Original Sin—but once you reject the idea of Original Sin, all you do is open the gates to it and all its cultural manifestations. A bland, naïve, secular humanitarianism is not Christianity. Christianity certainly must manifest itself in humane acts. But a humanitarianism that is separated from the realities of the human condition—that rejects both heroic virtue and the reality of sin—becomes antisocial and self-destructive.

This kind of secular humanism in the political form of liberalism has been called "Christianity without the Cross." The golden mean led the noble minds of the past to understand, to one degree or another, the exercise of virtue. But it ultimately leads to the Cross, for the Cross is the ultimate balance between good and evil, between light and dark. This is the message that Christ came into the world to give. It is the message He displayed on the Cross, and it is the message that He empowered us to spread throughout the world through His Resurrection and Ascension and the gift of the Holy Spirit at Pentecost.

We are not engaged in obscure antiquarianism when we talk of the classical minds of the past. When we do this, we really are manifesting the simple fact that we are civilized people—that is, people who have inherited a civilization and who have a duty to pass it on. Nothing that is true, such as the concept of the golden mean, should be so alien to us.

Whether people lived a generation ago, a thousand years ago, or even if their names were Adam and Eve, they all shared the human condition. Over time, civilizations have learned that we have to live according to the divine design implanted in creation. When we do that, it is called virtue.

We can do it on our own to some degree, by our own cultivation of the experiences of the past and our own discipline of our lower nature. But we need something else, and that is grace. Grace is the gift of God that makes the natural virtues, struggling to live the golden mean, willing to follow that road all the way to Jerusalem and up the hill to Christ on the Cross, who is the Golden Mean Himself. Jesus says, "If any man would come after me, let him deny himself and take up his cross daily and follow me" (Luke 9:23).

All those voices of antiquity longed to hear those words and that voice. Most of them did not hear it, and when the rest of them did, they were confused. But on this side of the Cross and the Resurrection, we have no excuse for being confused by Christ or for rejecting Him. In every age, there is a choice given to us. Voices from the past give us clues to God—but God Himself in Christ gives us grace and truth. If we want to begin living seriously the golden mean, we have to make one solid commitment: to live a life of virtue—and, by all means, to avoid mediocrity.

2

The Wages of Deceit

or

How Lies Turn Us Away from God

I don't think I'm telling tales out of school when I say that our schools are not what they should be. And that's putting it mildly. I think the state of education in the United States, on the whole, is in meltdown.

Twenty percent of all Americans recently indicated that they thought that we had landed a man on Mars. That is the kind of distance from reality that governs much public perception. In another survey, this one in the State University of New York system, the vast majority of graduating seniors could not pass the test that is given to immigrants seeking United States citizenship. These are not arcane subjects, but basic historical literacy, such as the date of the Declaration of Independence and the name of the first president. If we are so detached from recent shared experiences, it should not surprise us that the general public understanding of the human experience, broadly speaking, is practically nonexistent.

This has moral consequences, for we are the children of Adam and Eve. If we do not know that they walked this earth and fell for a terrible lie, we will live their lie as well. The prince of lies told our first ancestors that they could be as gods, and in accepting this lie, they entered into an imitation of reality where we are the focal point, the hinge on which reality bends. And when we live an imitation, we can no longer be at home with reality. Heaven is the ultimate reality, and if we lie and live a lie, we cannot be citizens of the eternal kingdom. That's why our first ancestors lost paradise.

Our society has come to take lying for granted. In fact, many people who lie in the public forum are admired for their cleverness in doing so. On the other hand, when a public figure is caught telling an inconvenient truth, we say that he has made a gaffe.

In the sixth chapter of the book of Proverbs is a list of things abominable to God, and one of them is lying (Prov. 6:17). God is truth. His Word is truth. He is the Truth itself. When He came into the world as Christ, He said it clearly: "I AM the Way and the Truth and the Life." The way to Heaven depends on our obedience to the truth of God. And our obedience to the truth of God, in turn, bestows eternal life. Without the truth, we lose our way—and we die.

Adam and Eve remain alive in us. Of course, St. Paul said, "It is no longer I who live, but Christ who lives in me" (Gal. 2:20). But Adam also lives in us in our fallen nature. As in Adam, all die, so in Christ, shall all be made alive. And unless the Adam in us is conquered by the Christ in us, the death of Adam is forever. That is damnation.

The twentieth century came to revere lies—not only to believe them, but to extol them, to admire them, and to celebrate them. Some of the most influential books of the twentieth century were anthologies of lies. In London, at beginning of that century, the naïve but prominent couple Beatrice and Sidney Webb set up in their house a little shrine to the man they thought was the prophet of the new age, Vladimir Lenin. Of course, they conveniently ignored the horrors he was perpetrating, the forced famines he was engineering, and the assassinations he was plotting. They were living a lie. Beatrice and Sidney Webb wrote one book after another claiming that Lenin's new order really was ushering in a workers' paradise.

Margaret Mead wrote a book that made her the prophet of modern anthropology. She, like Rousseau two centuries earlier, denied, for all practical purposes, the fallen nature of man, Adam's inheritance in our blood. She wrote about Samoa and the idyllic life led by the indigenous peoples before civilization corrupted them. Her own peers have since had to admit that she cooked her statistics and misrepresented what she saw.

And there was another Margaret, Margaret Sanger, who did far worse damage. She came to persuade a whole century that life is an enemy, that children are a threat to civilization, and that we alone are creators—not procreators with God, but the engineers of the human race. She employed and popularized the eugenic theories of the Nazis. She wrote lie upon influential lie, and today she is still revered by many.

Alfred Kinsey published surveys of men's and women's sexual behavior. It is now widely acknowledged that he lied. And yet what he wrote continues to be cited as some kind of biological gospel. Paul Ehrlich's *The Population Bomb* made numerous extravagant predictions about the decimation of the earth by overpopulation by the end of the twentieth century. Again, not only was he mistaken, but we now know he engaged in deliberate misinformation.

Other ages have spread misinformation, but the twentieth century specialized in disinformation—the intentional dissemination of lies—and that is far worse. There is something diabolical in the very word "disinformation." It really is a twin to moral death. For when the intellect turns on itself and uses its perception to contradict its purpose—namely, the spreading of truth—it becomes suicidal. The twentieth century, with all its achievements, nevertheless ended up confused and disappointed because it was still living the lie of Adam.

The Latin historian Suetonius wrote of the emperor Tiberius and his theological quandary. Tiberius reigned at the start of Christianity, and in fact, the Sea of Galilee was sometimes referred to by his name. He concluded that the pantheon of the gods that he had been taught as a child was fiction. Suetonius tells us that Tiberius looked at the stars in the heavens and consulted them, and he looked into the pantheon and found it vacant. That really is an analogy for the human condition at the end of the modern age. The problem is the people have not only lost heart in the false gods, but they have also been told that the True God doesn't exist. It is not only the pantheon that seems empty to them; it is the Church of God, and indeed the entire universe that has been voided.

Our Lord is Truth, and He settles for nothing but the truth. This, of course, caused much astonishment among those who heard Him. They remarked, "No man ever spoke like this man!" (John 7:46). No one ever told it the way it is, quite like He did. And yet most of them still preferred to live more comfortable lies. When you do that, you become a lie, and all the hope that God offers us disappears, and we dissolve into what can only be called fear. Oh, we may dress it up in more sophisticated language and call it angst or anxiety. But it is fear—the fear that there is a vast emptiness in the holy places and that the only way we can make sense of the world is by trying to read the motion of the stars like tea leaves. Superstition, not "reason," replaces true doctrine.

Louis XIV of France, as a young man, lived for a time in the Tuileries, attached to the Louvre Palace. Someone pointed out to him one day that on a clear day he could look out the window and see on the horizon the Church of St. Denis, which was the traditional burial church of the kings of France. This was no consolation to Louis. While he was baptized and reared a Catholic, in his heart of hearts, Adam was too much alive in him. After all, he was the Sun King, and he was unhappy to be reminded that only the Son of God is really a king and that all earthly rule derives from Him. Louis's solution was simple, but it was also a lie: He added a wing to the royal palace to block the view of the royal tombs.

This is again an allegory for the ennui of postmodern civilization. Busyness, distraction, amusement: We embrace these things to block out the fact of our mortality. And when we believe that lie, we participate in the oldest lie of all. If we think we are gods—if we alone define the space around us; if truth is only our perception; if one religion is as good as any other; or if I can get along without any religion beyond the exaltation of my desires—then I am living the old lie by which Adam fell: "You shall be as gods."

And that is why Jesus says that Satan was a liar from the beginning. He doesn't say that Satan lied through the Romans or the Greeks or the Pharisees. Satan lied from the very moment the first human appeared, for his very constitution is to contradict the divine will. Christ, then, was crucified because of lies. When He was taken before the Sanhedrin, witnesses contradicted themselves. They claimed that He had said that He would destroy the temple, but that was a clever and willful misrepresentation. What He said was, "Destroy this temple, and in three days I will raise it up" (John 2:19).

To live a lie is to be afraid of the truth. Why do we call the good thief on the cross next Christ "good"? It is simply because he was willing to overcome his fear and embrace the truth. He said, "This Man has done nothing wrong" (Luke 23:41). Measure those words. These aren't the words of a jury's acquittal. A jury will say only that the accused did not do what he was accused of doing. But the good thief says that Jesus of Nazareth *did nothing wrong*. That is an unprecedented statement. Even the pagans rarely dared to say that about their mythical gods. And the good thief did not even know that Jesus was the Incarnation of God, but he did know that He had done nothing wrong—and he had the courage to say so.

The Greeks told a story of the philosopher Diogenes, who represented the pursuit of truth, searching for an honest man. Diogenes walked through the streets with a lamp, looking for one honest man. Well, there is at least one famous painting of Christ holding a lamp, that by the Victorian artist Holman Hunt. Jesus is knocking on a door with vines growing up around it. This is the door of the soul, and Christ, His head pierced with the thorns, is holding a lamp, knocking, and seeking entry. This is the image of words related to us by John in Revelation: "Behold, I stand at the door and knock; if any one hears my voice and opens the door, I will come in to him and eat with him, and he with me" (Rev. 3:20). Jesus is searching for the honest soul in our civilization. He will be looking for the honest things we do, intermingled, yes, with all the lies we tell. He is looking for Himself, Who is displaced by Adam every time we sin.

But Jesus does not need the light; Jesus is the Light. And this completely changes all perception. From the beginning of time, before there was time, He is the Truth that chases away the darkness of deceit. But our society has lost heart for that truth. A spokesman for one highly placed political figure not long ago said that his boss had kept all the campaign promises he intended to keep. That is something that we have come to expect to hear, but what was most extraordinary was that so few people were offended by it, that so few people realized that it was a contradiction of personal dignity and the dignity of the human race.

Jesus is the Light of the World. He alone knows truth in its fullness. There are voices in our society today, however, that want the Church—the Body of Christ—to lie. They want the Church to water down the truths about God, how He has made the world, how He has saved the world, and how He moves through the Holy Spirit in His Holy Church. There are those who want to refashion the Church according to the Adam in them. But honest souls see through that.

The actor Alec Guinness, a convert to the Faith, said in his book *Blessings in Disguise* that the thing he regrets most in life is not having become a Catholic sooner. You might say that an actor makes a profession of lying, but that's really not what acting is about. Real acting is playing out the truths of life on the stage in symbolic form, in appropriated language, but all while serving the truth. And I think a great actor like Guinness realizes that the greatest drama of all is on no other stage but the stage of human history, and that there is no theme more compelling to an audience than the Passion and Resurrection of Christ. Certainly, the good thief knew that. God in His infinite mercy reminds us of that with great delicacy time and time again.

The story of Job is not as old as Adam's, but not by much. In the thirty-eighth chapter of Job, God says:

> Where were you when I laid the foundation of the earth? Tell me if you have understanding.... Have the gates of death been revealed to you, or have you seen the gates of deep darkness? Have you comprehended the expanse of the earth? Declare, if you know all this. (Job 38:4, 17–18)

He says the same to us at the end of what we vainly call "the modern age."

All we have to do to get rid of the old Adam and to embrace the new Christ is to say the most honest thing that a thief ever said, "This Man has done nothing wrong." And when anyone criticizes Christ, when anyone blasphemes His Holy Church, when anyone snubs the saints, ask them, "What have they really done wrong?

What did Christ do that was wrong? And what is He doing now that is wrong?" It is the world that lies against Christ, but when we say that He has done nothing wrong, then He will say to us what Adam longed to hear, "This day, you will be with me in Paradise" (Luke 23:43).

3

Innocent Blood

or

How Contempt for Innocence Deadens Faith and Love

There are two ways to write history. One is to write as you are living it—the eyewitness account. The narrative poems of the Greeks and the Romans were precisely that. They could smell the battles, and they had met the people. Firsthand experience tells the truth, as much as we can tell the truth mingled with our own prejudices.

But the other way to tell the history is to wait to gain perspective from time and distance. As an artist steps back to survey the canvas, so must a few generations pass in order for one to be able to tell the story of an age more expansively. I suppose this is why figures of historical interest tend to fade away in the public eye for a period as soon as they die. The initial fascination is gone, and we have to digest who they were, what they did, and what they meant.

Whenever some telling analysis of the twentieth century is written, whether of a political, economic, philosophical, or, above all, theological nature, it would likely be written on a computer, for the twentieth century gave us the computer. But it would be even more appropriate, we must say, for it to be written in blood.

Grace and Truth

The twentieth century saw more bloodshed than all other ages combined. When we regard the record of accomplishments in that extraordinary hundred years, we can easily be dazzled by the gifts, the inventions, the insights, and how the age was able to communicate these things. At the same time, we must wonder how it was that so much good could have mingled with so much blood.

Just look at the statistics. In China alone, as far as can be estimated, some 60 million people were killed. In the Soviet Union, it was over 20 million. In Cambodia, 2 million, which in proportion to the population represented the worst genocide in human history. Another 2 million were killed in North Korea, at least a million in Eastern-Central Europe, 1.7 million in Africa, 1.5 million in Afghanistan, and over 150,000 in Latin America. All these figures, by the way, are *apart from* the world wars. Rather, they refer to murders committed in the name of the most lurid denial of God, Marxism.

To deny God is to deny life. Jesus is the Way and the Truth and the Life. To deny Christ, therefore, is to usher in the shedding of blood. Those statistics shocked the world when they were published by the French writer Stéphane Courtois, in *The Black Book of Communism*. How could we be shocked after having lived through it? By the end of the century, we were used to the shedding of blood—but large portions of our society denied the malignancy of institutionalized atheism. Marxism was looked upon as an experiment motivated by benign intention, and when it showed its evil hand, many pseudo-sophisticates looked the other way.

In the sixth chapter of Proverbs, among the things listed that are abominable to God is the shedding of innocent blood (Prov. 6:17). There is a distinction made there between the shedding of blood generally and the shedding of *innocent* blood. It is the distinction between killing and murder. There are times, for instance, in self-defense, or in noble wars fought with right intention that, as St. Thomas Aquinas says, one is morally derelict if one does not fight—and that fighting may consequentially involve the shedding of blood. But the shedding of innocent blood is another matter.

God is the Author of life. We cannot create; we can only procreate. As the stewards of creation, we pass on life biologically, and morally we cultivate the intellect and the will of the soul. Because the human being is made in the image of God, and capable by an act of the will of loving Him Who loves us, all human dignity rests in reverence for the innocence of life.

We have inherited the tendency to rebel against the Lord of life. St. Paul analyzes himself: "For I do not do the good I want, but the evil I do not want is what I do.... Wretched man that I am!" (Rom. 7:19, 24). But he doesn't leave it at that. With a spirit of great joy, hope, and faith, St. Paul realizes and declares that Christ can get him out of that bind: "Who will deliver me from this body of death? Thanks be to God through Jesus Christ our Lord!" (Rom. 7:24–25).

The ability to procreate life goes hand in hand with the ability to shed blood. The state is invested with a special responsibility to protect life and to promote the tranquility of order. And, on occasion, that involves the use of disciplines to deter and to punish those who do shed innocent blood. The authority of the state to make these difficult decisions, even sometimes to the point of life and death, is not given by any ecclesial power. It is given by God Himself.

Therefore, as Jesus says to Pontius Pilate, "You would have no power over me unless it had been given you from above" (John 19:11). Our Lord does not deny Pilate's right to execute, but He tells him that power does not originate with him or even with Caesar in Rome. It comes from Heaven, from the same God Who gives us the gift of life. And therefore, when the state exercises its authority over life and death, it must be, above all, guided by the truth of the sacredness of life.

There was an interesting man, a Maestro Titto in the nineteenth century who lived into his eighties, as the official papal executioner. Very few people know about him today, but he was very well known in his day. He personally executed 516 people in the Papal States, in the exercise of justice. He largely did this during the pontificate of Pius IX, who is now being declared *beatus*, a Blessed. This should indicate to us that the exercise of capital punishment is not *malum in se*, as is the shedding of innocent blood. In other words, it is not evil by its very existence. But it can be twisted. It can be perverted. And the highest authorities in the Church remind us today that it is of such a solemn order and is exercised in a society so contemptuous of life that we must be very judicious indeed in its exercise.

But one muddies the water if one equates a legitimate exercise of this power with the shedding of innocent blood. How ironic it is that some of the voices most outspoken against executing murderers also promote contraception, abortion, and euthanasia. They are living a contradiction of God's plan; they have defied holy innocence. And that's why shedders of innocent blood have to use the language of deceit—that is, euphemisms. Abortionists are called "health-care providers." Well, that's like calling an ax murderer a cutlery specialist. And people who promote abortion say they are "pro-choice." All that manifests, besides their own guilt, is bad grammar. "To choose" is a transitive verb; it needs an object. The "pro-choice" person must finish the sentence: choice of what?

The great twentieth-century theologian Hans Urs von Balthasar said that "everywhere outside of Christianity, the child is automatically sacrificed."[3] That is not hyperbole: History shows it to

---

[3] *Wenn ihr nicht werdet wie dieses Kind* (Ostfildern bei Stuttgart: Schwabenverl., 1988).

be true. Whenever the dignity of the human person, founded in the redemptive power of Christ, is ignored, the selfish pride of man will find some excuse to attack innocence. With an indescribable sorrow from the Cross, Our Lord saw innocent life being shattered from the beginning to the very end of time. All the body parts of the fifty million babies who have been killed in the United States—those were before His eyes. And at the very beginning of the human race, Cain slew Abel. God said to Cain, "The voice of your brother's blood is crying to me from the ground" (Gen. 4:10). When the population of the world was one household, it was clearer that each one of us is a brother or a sister to one another. As time has moved on, though, it has become easier to reduce people to statistics. But God never looks upon us as a statistic.

There is a kind of schizophrenia that a world buys into when it has lost its reverence for innocence. The very so-called civilized people who speak about legalizing the shedding of innocent blood will speak of "child welfare." In State of the Union addresses we are almost always told that the state of our country has never been better. I am not qualified to analyze that in detail, but I do know enough about history to know that when someone says that kind of thing, our ears should perk up. In 1912, the *Titanic* was declared an unsinkable ship. In the 1930s, we were guaranteed peace in our time. This is not the language of innocence; it is the language of naïveté.

Naïveté is the world's substitute for innocence. True Innocence came into the world as Christ. True Innocence hung on the Cross. And by the shedding of His blood, He was able to bring innocence back into the world. That's really what it means to be born again.

4

The Sin of Intrigue

or

How to Keep the Imagination Trained on God

The word "intrigue" can refer to two different phenomena. The first is simple fascination. Certainly no one who ever lived was more intriguing than Jesus of Nazareth. He intrigued those who saw and heard Him in His own day, and He continues to intrigue. Movies and television and print media try to capitalize on this intrigue — often in stupid and sensationalistic ways — but the truth remains that people are drawn to Him. We will never understand Jesus, however, if He only intrigues us in this way. The saints understood this; they were and are never merely fascinated with Jesus. He is not a celebrity to them. He is life itself. When the divine light of Christ transfigures the soul, it raises the virtues to a higher, even heroic degree. This, not mere fascination, is the content of holiness: the integrity of the personality, becoming the person one is really supposed to be.

But there is a second kind of intrigue. And that, says the book of Proverbs, is an abomination to God (6:18). This fascination is not harmless or morally neutral, and it certainly is not the first

25

level of an approach to God. It is really rejection of God and His goodness. This kind of intrigue, condemned by the rabbis and then by the prophets and the Fathers of the Church, is the devising of wicked imaginings, the distortion of the imaginative faculty to plot against God.

The whole Passion narrative of Christ is a drama of that kind of intrigue. When He was preaching, people began to plot how they could capture Him. When He proclaimed His Messiahship in His native synagogue in Nazareth, the crowd tried to grab Him and throw Him off the brow of a hill. It was not yet His time, and He escaped from their midst.

The human intellect is a gift from God, and it must be used as He intended—to glorify Him. The imaginative component of the intellect can remember the past and can anticipate the future. And so the imagination can civilize us by collecting and organizing the inheritance left by those who have gone before—their stories and wisdom and experience. And it can encourage us through contemplation of what we can build, what we can design, what we can hope for. But that same imagination can turn in on itself. We can be haunted by the past. We can be threatened by the future. And we can use its power for destructive purposes.

When Our Lord was taken before Pontius Pilate, the crowd cried out what no Jewish voice in Jerusalem had ever said before: "We have no king but Caesar" (John 15:19). This unprecedented surrender to civil authority over the power of the Lord of Israel was clearly the result of the misuse of the imaginative faculty—that is, an intriguing against God. Pontius Pilate and Herod also intrigued between themselves: They became friends as they plotted against Christ to cement their own power.

If you go through the Passion narratives, you can identify every personality that has ever lived. All the foibles of the human race are on display in one character or another. We cannot look at these characters as though they are somehow distinct from us, for in every one of them is a part of our own soul. God has given us the Passion narratives, edited by the Holy Spirit, so that we can have the anecdotes and dialogues and characters He wants us to know. This heavenly script is an examination of conscience for us and our ego's intrigues against the divine design.

Jesus says, "I am the Way, the Truth, and the Life." But the ego resists that, and that's why we can look for two thousand years at the Way Himself and still find ourselves wandering away from Him. After two thousand years, we can look the Truth straight in the face and still lie about Him. After two thousand years, we can look at the Lord of life and still fall prey to the conceit that life is just a biological accident.

The Greeks had a parable about the dangers of the autonomous ego in the story of Narcissus. Narcissus was fascinated with himself. Now, it can be healthy to be fascinated with yourself. The child spends the first several months of his life aware of practically nothing but the self, discovering his own parts, his mechanism for living. This is part of natural growth. But there comes a moment when the infant becomes aware of the world around him. The word "idiot" really means someone who is totally aware of the self and only the self, oblivious to the other—other people, the outside world, and the Holy Other Who is God.

Narcissus was that kind of moral idiot. He became enamored of his reflection in the water. He wanted to discover, in the jargon of our day, his "inner child." But anyone who wants to find his inner child without locating the source of life in God is condemned to a perpetual infancy, an arrested development of the soul. The autonomous self ignores the voice of the other, all others. And so it was with Narcissus, for Echo called to him, bidding him to come and be her lover. Narcissus was so involved with himself that her voice fell, literally, on morally deaf ears. She dissolved into nothing but her voice, which is how we get the word "echo." Narcissus ended up dissolving into a plant that is named for him.

The pathology of modern man has consisted in that kind of moral deafness to God, a self-centeredness that is born of intrigue. When we plot, according to our own devices, to reorder the world according to our own preferences, self-interest, and self-love, we ignore the voice of God. Our Lord says, "But to what shall I compare this generation? It is like children sitting in the market places and calling to their playmates, 'We piped to you, and you did not dance; we wailed, and you did not mourn'" (Matt. 11:16–17). What is wicked about intrigue, then, is a self-idolatry that demotes God, or blocks Him out entirely.

When Our Lord went to the Cross, He displayed, for everyone who had intrigued against Him, the sublime fact that the Light of the World had come into the world. Even more, that Light was willing to endure a moral darkness so that the world might understand Who He is, why He made the world, and how He remakes it. He cried, "My God! My God, why have You forsaken me?" (see Matt. 27:46), even though He had said that He is never alone. Heaven was in Him even in that most desolate moment. But as He cried out, He took on the burden of a mankind who had so intrigued against their own God that He, the Christ, begins to lose a grasp on Who God is and what the soul is. Jesus always called God His Father, but in this moment, God began to become merely an abstraction.

That's the problem with intrigue and the misuse of the imagination. When we try to defy the mystery of God, when we try to reorder it according to the lights of our limited intellect, then He becomes a gauzy abstraction; He virtually disappears. Our Lord has given us the purpose to serve Him on earth and to give Him delight so that we might be with Him in glory forever. That's very difficult to understand and to live out, if you have interpreted the world according to your own definition of the way to live, of the biological and moral constitution of life, and of truth itself.

We can't afford lapses into intrigue because we are engaged all the time in the spiritual warfare of the soul. St. Peter knew all about that war: He had become a casualty of it by denying Christ. He gave in to a certain kind of intrigue when he sat by the fire and said, "I do not know him" (Luke 22:57). But in humility Peter recovered the right use of his imagination. As the Prince of the Apostles, he wrote to the early Christian churches, telling them, "Be sober, be watchful. Your adversary the devil prowls around like a roaring lion, seeking some one to devour. Resist him, firm in your faith" (1 Pet. 5:8–9). That warning has been part of the Night Prayer of the Church for centuries, appropriately designated to be read when darkness has fallen and we are tempted to think that the Light of Christ is hidden. You can almost hear the paws of the lion roaming about the soul.

Satan, after all, is the great intriguer. All human intrigues pale in comparison with his great intrigue against Christ. The worst crimes humans have ever committed in history are mere playthings compared with the vicious scheming of the prince of lies against the Lord of Truth. And here's the thing: He wants us to become part of his intrigue. In our current generation, he wants us to use all the scientific information and communication technology at our hands to perpetuate his plotting against the divine design. He wants us to think that we have no home but our earthly dwelling. He wants us to think that there is no heavenly purpose to our existence.

After Theodore Roosevelt left the White House, he went on a safari in Africa and toured Europe. He was wined and dined, given honorary degrees, and returned to his native city of New York, where he was welcomed with great pageantry. On the ship with him were two missionaries who had spent many years in laborious service for the Gospel and the salvation of souls. When they saw all the acclamation given to Roosevelt, one said to the other, "They don't even know we exist." And the other replied, "But we are not yet home."

Each one of us has a home with God. And the only way we can make sense of our earthly home, the only way we can properly use our advanced technology, and the only way we can really know what to say and to do with all our means of communication is to understand that we have a heavenly destiny. If we plot and intrigue against God, we will become the first casualties in our spiritual battle. For if life has no purpose, then there is no reason for us to put up with the challenges of everyday life. The slothful soul easily surrenders to the ennui that has become the undercurrent of our fading modern age. Our Lord does not condemn us for the mistakes we have made in this culture, nor for the sins we have committed by our intellect and our will. What He does do, however, is judge how we pick ourselves up, remonstrate with Him for His grace and mercy, and go back out to proclaim that He is the Way, the Truth, and the Life.

In the Second World War, the entire fate of Europe and, consequently, Western civilization hung in the balance. Winston Churchill was one of those characters in history who are hard to explain apart from divine providence. It's not that he was a mystic or a great confessor of the Faith or a saint raised to the altars, but that he was a man with all the gifts needed for that moment in order to resist the denial of God instituted in a political system.

It is said that in some of the darkest days of the Second World War, he would go out into the garden at 10 Downing Street with his cigar and sing in an unmelodious voice a number that had been popularized by the Scottish vaudeville singer Harry Lauder. In those dark days, Churchill knew that across the Channel there was an evil man and an evil system intriguing against God, and so he walked around the garden singing this simple song: "Keep right on to the end of the road. Keep right on to the end. Though the way be long, let your heart be strong. Keep right on to the end. If you are tired and weary, still journey on till you come to your happy abode, where all you love and you're dreaming of will be there at the end of the road."

Our Lord told us just that two thousand years ago. He said to the Apostle Philip what he says to us now at the end of a long period of intriguing against God by civilization in the West and in the East, "Have I been with you so long, and yet you do not know me?" (John 14:9).

5

The Propensity to Do Evil

or

How We Redefine the Good to Justify Our Sins

I remember a political debate where participants were asked, "Who is your favorite philosopher?" It is quite amazing, in today's day and age, that most of them were able to come up with any answers at all. But to their credit, they did volunteer.

Mostly their answers were ones you'd expect — Aristotle, Plato and so on. But one piously said that his favorite philosopher was Jesus. Another replied with even greater rectitude that Jesus was not a philosopher: Jesus is not a lover of wisdom, but Wisdom itself. He is the Truth that has ordered the universe. Philosophy is a natural activity of the mind — the discerning of the basic hierarchy of principles by which we deduce what truth is. Theology, however, moves beyond philosophy by considering the source of truth itself.

When Our Lord was twelve years old, the rabbis in the temple marveled at His wisdom. I am sure that Our Lady and St. Joseph had a very good little domestic school going in Nazareth, but His wisdom did not come from them. In His human nature, He did have to learn natural things; for instance, He had to be taught the grammar of the Scriptures that He had given the world. But this magnificent paradox does not contradict His divine nature, which is not merely intelligent, but is the source of all intelligence.

We have discussed several of the abominations listed in the sixth chapter of Proverbs, including intrigue, plotting, wicked imaginings, and twisting the intellect. But after we have imagined things, after we have plotted against God, there is a readiness to act upon that disobedience. Abominable in the eyes of God, then, is a readiness to do evil.

The human being has a free will to choose good or evil. But after having plotted evil, when a person begins to commit the act itself, it begins to contradict the human dignity and the conscience in a more poignant way. This is why the most evil people in the world have had to redefine evil, pretending that it was good. Or, when that hasn't worked, they have had to drug themselves, either with intoxicating language — slurs and euphemisms and so on — or with chemical drugs. How paradoxical it is that an age such as ours, which claims to be so committed to reason and realism, should really become a drug culture, but it is no puzzle. If we cooperate with evil, if we plot to do evil, and then if we commit ourselves to evil, the human spirit has to deny that what it is doing is evil. Evil always calls itself good; every vice parades itself as a form of liberation.

In the nineteenth century there was a remarkable character named Fr. Theobald Mathew, an Irish Capuchin who dedicated his life to the temperance movement. There are those today who speak patronizingly of such work, but he was not a puritanical teetotaler, and drunkenness truly was a social crisis at that time. He had a higher vision, a vision of the human soul as a reflection of the glory of God. And it was so wonderful to him that he wanted people to understand that they were losing sight of something far more splendid than what alcohol or any drug could give.

He was a virtual miracle worker, giving the temperance pledge to hundreds of thousands of Irish and, on one occasion, to a multitude of a hundred thousand Scotsmen. He came to the United States and visited at the White House, where he presented his work to the admiration of President Zachary Taylor. The vice president at the time, who later became President Millard Fillmore, received him at City Hall in New York, and it is said that he even took the pledge.

What Fr. Mathew faced in his day was no different from the drug culture we face today. Any sociologist can come up with an explanation for why alcohol was such a problem in the nineteenth century: The breakdown of social institutions, economic oppression, the suppression of religion, political tyranny, or any number of other things drove people to seek some kind of escape. But this good priest told the people that God gives us not an escape but an "inscape"—a vision of the good that challenges every attempt to contradict that good by doing evil.

Our Lord gives us His Body and His Blood in the Holy Eucharist. When the world denies the majestic reality of the Holy Eucharist, it will always try to drink itself into oblivion or drug itself out of reality. Any attempt to redefine the Blessed Sacrament as something less than the sacrifice of Christ for the forgiveness of sins and the presentation on the altar of His True Body, Blood, Soul, and Divinity is an embarkation upon a kind of semi-life.

Why do people even consider doing evil? Well, it's in the blood —not the Blood of Christ, but human nature. It's Original Sin. When we appropriate that Original Sin in the form of explicit acts against the good, that's what we call a sin. Our Lord told a parable about the owner of a vineyard who left tenants in charge of the land. The proprietor sent one man to visit the vineyard and collect the rents, and that man was beaten. Another went to the vineyard, and he was gravely wounded. And then finally he said, "Surely, they will not touch my son." He sent his son in, and they killed him.

Grace and Truth

Our Lord is giving us an allegory for sin. The beating of the first servant is venial sin, a lighter kind of offense against the good that can easily be remedied through an Act of Contrition. It does not even require a sacramental Confession, though it is recommended. But a venial sin is not to be dismissed lightly, because it lays the groundwork for the more direct affront against God represented by the wounding of the other servant, which represents habitual sin. The ache in the soul that takes away our desire for the good forms a habit of behavior. These habits lead to the gravest offense of all: killing of the Son Himself. This is mortal sin, and every mortal sin is an act of violence against the Lord of Life. St. John Vianney said that when we confess our sins, we take the nails out of Jesus.

Charles Darwin, in his expedition to the Galapagos Islands, noted with great insight how the wildlife seemed unperturbed by the arrival of his ship or the men on it. The reason was clear: They had never seen humans before, and thus had no reason to feel threatened by them. They were not potential hunters or collectors, but just like the birds in the air and the beasts of the field. But, he observed, the seals jumped off the rocks and swam away at the ship's approach, for the seals alone of all the species on that island had a long experience of being hunted by humans.

The sons of Adam were like those seals. We have had a long experience — that is, all of human history — to observe and to learn the various ways in which people have offended God by offending against men and women, and this has created a deep wound in the human heart. If we are not careful, it can rust into cynicism, which denies the possibility of holiness and eternal joy. Cynicism cooperates with evil.

One of the most admirable writers in the English language was Jonathan Swift. He lived something of a misplaced life as a non-Celt living in Ireland and the dean of the Protestant cathedral of a Catholic country. But he was a man of deep natural virtue. He saw injustice all around him, and he marshaled his literary talent to do what he could to publicize these accounts. To do this, he unleashed his acidic tongue in the form of biting satire.

A lot of people continue to think that Swift's *Gulliver's Travels* is a children's book. It is anything but! A child can enjoy it, of course, but it was written for the minds and hearts of the most sophisticated people of his day. He aimed his satirical barbs at the government officials and the representatives of the ancient institutions of his culture who had fallen into the dismal self-parody of worshipping themselves and their class instead of worshipping the God Who gave them life and power and prosperity.

He reserved particular scorn for the intellectuals who used their intelligence for no useful purpose at all. In the book, they live on a flying island, which they can never quite get to settle down on solid ground. He satirizes the politicians as jumping through hoops or over strings just to get a particular kind of colored ribbon. Swift laid before the reader how easy it is for us, deprived of the vision of God, to lapse into a kind of innocent rejection of our own dignity. Once we have done that, we become easy prey for the liar. The prince of lies knows that once we have lost the vision of higher things, we can be persuaded to participate in the lower things.

Jonathan Swift, as I said, was a man of natural virtue, to a remarkable degree. What he did lack were the theological virtues of faith, hope, and love to a degree that could overcome bitterness and cynicism. He practically dissolved in his frustration and indignation at the injustices of his day. On his tomb in the cathedral in Dublin is this epitaph: "Where savage indignation no longer tears his heart apart."

Our Lord doesn't want us to deny that kind of bittersweet indignation, but He also doesn't want our hearts to be torn apart by cynicism. The goodness of the human soul can discern good from evil, but it will be eternally frustrated if it doesn't have access to the grace and truth of Christ, which can release the good and conquer the evil.

It is highly significant that Our Lord reveals Himself as an eternal light shining in the darkness. Our Lord, when He wanted us to see His divine mercy, showed it in a private revelation to St. Faustina with lights coming out of Him. The Light that made the world can cancel out the propensity to evil that is in every human heart.

Instead of surrendering to indignation and dying with a sense of futility, it is far better to follow the example of the saints. In particular, we could take as our model that saint whose very name means "fire": Ignatius Loyola. He prayed in his *Spiritual Exercises*, and the Church has taken up his prayer ever since,

Take, O Lord, and receive my entire liberty, my memory, my understanding, and my will. All that I am and have You have given to me. And I give all back to You to be disposed of according to Your good pleasure. Give me only the comfort of Your presence and the joy of Your love, and with these, I shall be more than rich and shall desire nothing more.

6

Humility and Honesty

or

How We Witness to the Perfection of Christ

As Our Lord was about to go to the Cross, He prayed to His Father in Heaven, "I glorified you on earth, having accomplished the work that you gave me to do" (see John 17:4). It might seem like an astonishing thing for anyone to say—and especially someone who defines the virtue of humility. But humility dispenses with modesty. A truly humble man who is six feet tall doesn't, in a spirit of false modesty, say that he is only five foot eight.

We take delight when our projects come out right because we have all experienced doing things badly. I have a hobby of sketching, and there are times when I have been pleased with what I have drawn—but I also have closets full of mistakes. It is the second-rate carpenter who does not notice the cracks; the first-rate carpenter is as aware of the defects as he is of the apparent perfection in his work. It is the second-rate philosopher who overlooks his logical mistakes; the first-rate philosopher learns from his mistakes how to get things right.

Grace and Truth

But not one person has been able to say to the perfect King, "I glorified you on earth, having accomplished the work that you gave me to do." And indeed, in another context, the people affirmed Him with astonishment: "He has done all things well" (Mark 7:37). They were accustomed, as we all are, to imperfect people. And in fact, just as we do, they preferred imperfect people: Others' flaws excuse our own, all while we imagine that our peculiar imperfections are themselves a subtle kind of perfection. And so many of those who heard and observed Our Lord fled. More would have stayed, if He had told them the lies about Himself and themselves that they wanted to hear, for in their eyes, Christ's real offense was that He was not a blank slate upon which they could write their own ideas. He was the Truth, and that Truth was inescapable. One either embraced it or fled from it.

There is a school of philosophy called idealism. It doesn't mean reaching for the highest and best, but rather believing that something is true simply because it is your idea. The French have glorified Western civilization in many ways over the centuries, but since at least the time of Descartes, many French thinkers have placed more confidence in their pet theories than in demonstrable facts. It is said that a typical French philosopher will ask, "That may be true in practice, but how is it in theory?"

For two thousand years, the world has been tempted to deal with Christ that way—to say that He did wonderful things but that the moral and spiritual theory behind His practice just doesn't work. The Trinity doesn't work. The whole idea of the Word Made Flesh doesn't work. Would it not be better to let Him be the humanitarian, the reformer, the social liberator and leave it at that? But Our Lord did not come into the world to be merely a humanitarian or a reformer or a social liberator. He came to reconcile earth and Heaven. That is why He said that He had accomplished the work His Father had given him to do: He has let the world see God.

Our Lord came into the world to do all things well, and He did so. The Lord tells us that among the things that are abominable in His eyes is an intellectual conceit called bearing false witness — against our neighbor and ultimately against Him (Prov. 6:19). One way our modern culture is particularly adept at doing that is by denying the existence of truth itself. If we make God an abstraction, we have freed ourselves to create our own idol. Therefore, to say that Christ is not Christ — to say He is only a humanitarian, to say He is only a reformer, to say He is only a liberator, to say He is as close to perfection as could be but not perfection itself — that is to bear false witness against reality and against the God Who made and did all things well.

Living an abstraction by bearing false witness against the truth inevitably causes an emptiness in the soul. We know that there is something wrong with emptiness; there is an instinct in everyone to fill a void. Some time ago, Leonardo da Vinci's *Mona Lisa* was stolen from the Louvre. In the weeks between the theft and the painting's recovery, when the wall was blank, more people went to the Louvre Museum to see the empty space than went when the painting was there.

I suppose we could make that an analogy with the philosophical conceits of our modern age. The philosophy of existentialism really was a fascination with emptiness, the creation of a myth that said that life is not really alive, that there is no purpose, that there is no dignity in the human condition apart from the simple fact of our existence. More dramatically, nihilism and anarchism were (and are) forms of fascination with emptiness.

Our Lord fills our emptiness with His Own Body and His Own Blood. He says in the Eucharistic dialogue in John's Gospel: "Unless you eat the flesh of the Son of man and drink his blood, you have no life in you" (John 6:53). His disciples, used to theory rather than fact, accustomed to abstract ceremonies instead of something so basic as the Body and Blood of the Messiah, responded: "This is a hard saying" (John 6:60). Jesus then asserted, "But there are some of you that do not believe," which the Gospel writer comments is in reference to the one who would betray Him (John 6:64).

This man, Judas, followed Our Lord as though He were a theory. Judas confected his own mental image of what the Messiah should be: a humanitarian, yes; a reformer, yes; a political liberator, yes—but not the Son of God, the Word Made Flesh, the Redeemer crucified on a Cross for the wiping away of sins and the reconciliation between man and God. And so he walked away.

There are those who call themselves fundamentalists, who with the best of intentions take words of Scripture and decide on their own what they mean. These interpretations always conform to their pre-existing prejudices. (This is why fundamentalists really miss the fundamentals.) They might accept Baptism, because it is mentioned in the Scripture, but according to their lights it is only a kind of initiation ceremony. The Church has taught us, however, because Jesus says we must be born again of water and the Spirit, that the sacrament of Baptism has a regenerating effect.

So, too, the fundamentalist might reject the sacrament of Confession. But Our Lord said to the Apostles when He had risen from the dead: "Receive the Holy Spirit. If you forgive the sins of any, they are forgiven; if you retain the sins of any, they are retained" (John 20:22–23). And yet this economy of grace, the manifestation of God's mercy through the sacrament of Reconciliation does not fit the fundamentalist's theory of the way God is supposed to work.

Indeed, it is very difficult, looking back upon the experience of Christian history, to understand why God made the Church the way He did, why He structured it around the apostolic succession with the papacy as the central governing, confirming, and consoling voice of the Church. And yet Our Lord said to Peter, "On this rock, I will build my Church" (Matt. 16:18). It may not fit our theory of the way things should be, and yet Our Lord made it that way.

The Church's teaching about human life, especially with regard to abortion and euthanasia and contraception, doesn't fit the modern theory of the way the world is supposed to work. It doesn't fit the temper of the times. And yet respect for life is one of the things that Our Lord was thinking about when He said that He had done His Father's work: He manifested to us the dignity of life from the moment of conception. If we deny these things, we are bearing false witness—false witness against our human dignity, as well as against our God.

Our Lord was crucified by people bearing false witness. Annas, who had been high priest from 6 B.C. to A.D. 15, listened to Our Lord and saw a truth in Him that apparently unsettled him. He turned Our Lord over to his son-in-law Caiaphas, who was high priest in that year. And before Caiaphas came bearers of false witness. Mark says that one accuser quoted Our Lord as having said, "I will destroy this temple" (Mark 14:58). What Our Lord truly said was: "Destroy this temple, and in three days I will raise it up" (John 2:19).

Perfection unsettles imperfection. There is a strange notion that the more perfect someone is, the less human he is, but that is like saying that the more cracks there are in a window, the more of a window it is. Our Lord is true man and true God; His humanity is displayed in His perfection. In Him, for the first time, we saw what a man should be and can be. When we say "can be," we have proof: every saint who has lived in each generation. And each one of them has been subject, one way or another, to calumny, misrepresentation, false witness.

Consider the Irish bishop St. Oliver Plunkett. In 1681, he was accused by an ex-Franciscan of treason, a charge for which he was executed. Sometime after that, the man who had borne false witness against the saint had the audacity to call upon a priest. Whenever people lie against Christ and His saints, they do seem to grow in boldness. The priest excused himself for a moment and came back with a box. He opened it, and inside was the head of Oliver Plunkett. Needless to say, even that man was human enough to shrink away.

In 1955, the bishop of Shanghai, Ignatius Kung, was arrested by the Chinese Communists and taken into an arena, where he was put on the platform and instructed before thousands of his fellow Christians to deny the pope and the Catholic Church. The bishop of Shanghai, who was little more than five feet tall, reached up to the microphone and shouted, "Long live Christ the King! Long live the pope!" He was dragged away, and false witnesses accused him of treason — but his only treason was his loyalty to God. He spent thirty years in prison in one of those slow-motion martyrdoms of which we hear little. In March 2000 at the age of ninety-eight, Cardinal Kung — for he had been given the red hat by John Paul II secretly in 1979, then publicly in 1991 — went to his eternal reward. And when we speak of such a man as Cardinal Kung, we are not using a pious convention when we say that "he went to his eternal reward." Christ is faithful to those who bear faithful witness to Him.

In the book of Revelation, in the third chapter, God declares Himself "the faithful and true witness" (Rev. 3:14). If the world wants to live a lie, God will not be deterred from telling the truth. Every one of us will fail Him at some point. We have not done all things well as Christians. We know our mistakes, and we know how generation after generation has failed to match the glory of the spotless Bride of Christ.

But She is still the spotless bride. The Church is still the supernatural gift that Christ gives us from Heaven. The saints are witnesses to that — and we, in our better moments, are witnesses to that. However defective our acts may be, however frail and weak our prayers and the intentions of our petitions may be, whenever we talk to God in prayer, we end by saying, "Through Jesus Christ Our Lord." We do that because, while we are imperfect, He is perfect. And if we, with the solemn intention of the intellect and the will, offer our imperfections to Him, He joins them to His own offering of His very self when He says, "I glorified you on earth, having accomplished the work that you gave me to do."

7

Concord and Discord

or

How We Bring Harmony to Society and to Our Souls

There is a church on Park Avenue in New York City whose windows depict the Beatitudes. The Beatitude traditionally rendered "Blessed are the meek" is here translated "Blessed are the debonair." You might get the wrong impression, since this particular church is quite fashionable, but it's a good translation. It comes from an old French usage and means, "Blessed are those who have a good atmosphere in the soul." We might call this quality placidity, calmness, confidence, obsequiousness in the presence of God, a holy awareness that God is in charge — and it has been the mark of every saint in every culture.

One of the greatest men who ever lived was St. Louis IX, king of France in the thirteenth century. Louis represents all that was great and good about the High Middle Ages, which have been so misrepresented in recent times.

Louis's father died when his son was only twelve years old, and so the boy's mother, Blanche, became regent. She was the daughter of Alfonso of Castile and Eleanor of England, and she was an extraordinary woman in her own right. She once said she would rather have her son die than commit a single mortal sin. Louis was dearly devoted to his wife, Queen Margaret, though it was difficult for Margaret to get along with her exacting mother-in-law. He was the father of eleven children, who were utterly devoted to him, as he and his wife were to them. There was in the family and their court that debonair spirit.

Every aspect of culture felt his golden touch. In architecture, he gave us one of the most beautiful buildings in the world, the Sainte-Chapelle, as a shrine for what was believed to be Our Lord's crown of thorns. He cultivated reforms in the religious life, setting up several famous religious houses. In the administration of justice, he often listened to court cases himself. He was the court of last appeal, and people wanted to go before him because they knew he would rule justly. On one occasion, a young man was to be executed for treason for having participated in a rebellion led by his father. Louis refused to sentence him to death, saying, "It cannot be treason for a son to obey his father."

He supported the theologian Canon Robert de Sorbon in establishing a center of studies that we know as the University of Paris, or the Sorbonne. For his charity, he was celebrated throughout Europe. He regularly served a dozen beggars at his table, and he established what is believed to be the first hospital for the blind.

He also took the cross; that is, he enlisted in the Crusades. And it was on crusade in North Africa that he died, alongside his son, of typhoid. On August 24, 1270, at the age of fifty-six, St. Louis received the Last Sacraments. As he was dying, one of his final acts was to summon the Greek ambassadors and plead with them for the healing of the schism that had divided the Byzantine and the Latin churches. The next day, he lost his speech until noon, when he began to pray from the Psalms: "Lord, I will enter thy house. I will give thanks to thee in thy temple. And I will give glory to thy name" (Ps. 138:2, KJV). For the next three hours, just as Our Lord hung on the Cross from noon till three, he endured his last agony and then he uttered his last words: "Into Thy hands, I commend my spirit." That was a king. That was a man. "Blessed are the debonair."

The saints are walking examples of "concord," a word we use to describe peace of the soul and the peace between nations. It literally means a harmony of hearts: There can be peace only when hearts agree. And the Sacred Heart of Christ is the root of all peace.

The opposite of concord is discord, the separating of hearts. While in literature and psychology we always associate peace with light, where there is discord there is darkness. Wherever there is war, there is a foreboding sense that the light is going out. At the beginning of the First World War, Lord Gray famously remarked that "the lights are going out all over Europe. We shall not see them again in our time." Discord also brings a darkness into the soul. St. Paul says, "If I ... have not love, I am a noisy gong or a clanging cymbal" (1 Cor. 13:1).

The saints remind us that there is such a thing as peace, but it is not what a facile society often presents as peace. There can be no real peace in any institution, in any family, in any soul, without a meekness before God, without a good fellowship, a good spirit, a good atmosphere in the soul that is compatible with the harmony of Heaven.

The book of Proverbs tells us that the stirring up of discord is an abomination to God. That abomination comes into being in these three ways:

- *Denial of the natural law.* When we deny the natural law, we contradict the harmony of God's created order. We see this all the time in the contemporary world, in empty clichés such as: "A family is whatever you define a family to be"; "Marriage is only about who you love"; "Fetuses are just clumps of cells, not living human beings." Whenever we deny those basic principles of life, liberty, and the pursuit of happiness that are the foundational charisms of our country, we invite discord into the soul, into the family, into the nation, and into Christ's own Body, the Church.

• *Deification of the state.* It is part of God's will and design that there be a social institution for the promotion of the tranquility of order. But if the state does not conform to God's will, it voids its own legitimacy. The evolution of the concept of the state as an autonomous pole of authority took place over several centuries, reaching its most outrageous and cruel expression in the twentieth century in the forms of fascism and Marxism. We know the toll that was paid, and we know the discord of two world wars and countless other bloody conflicts.

• *Idolization of the body.* Just as the denial of natural law is an idolization of the ego, and the deification of the state is an idolization of the nation, so is the myth of biological perfection a deification of the organic fact of the body. This is expressed in eugenics, in social engineering in the form of contraception, and in every way that people understand their dignity in terms strictly of their body and their ability to manipulate it. Even the health and fitness fanatic can be guilty of this kind of idolatry. If people spend more time doing physical exercises than they do spiritual exercises, they have lapsed into this error.

These three idols have been identified and condemned by the Church, especially during the twentieth century. Pope Pius XI, just as the horror of the Second World War was about to cast its shadow upon the entire globe, issued an encyclical that he arranged to have smuggled into Germany: *Mit brennender sorge*, or "With burning zeal." What was he inflamed about? The denial of natural law; the deification of the state; and the myth of biological perfection, especially as the Nazis interpreted it in their pursuit of the "master race."

In that encyclical, he did not mention fascists or Nazis or Marxists by name. Some thought this was a deliberate oversight or neglect or worse. But Pius had a supernatural perception of the root of the problem of discord — and it applied well beyond the threats of that moment. Government systems come and go. He knew that the principal of discord, though, will always haunt civilization — and that is why what he wrote in 1937, words that were read from the pulpits of Germany, is so prophetic for our generation and for our nation.

That restless soul is palpable today. We deny natural law because we make our ego our god. We must "affirm" the self. But Our Lord in the Garden of the Agony said to His Father, "Not my will, but thine, be done" (Luke 22:42). The deification of the state creates the state as a god. But Our Lord said, "My Kingdom is not of this world" (John 18:36). And the myth of biological perfection deifies the flesh. But in the book of Job we read: "After my skin has been thus destroyed, then from my flesh I shall see God, whom I shall see on my side, and my eyes shall behold, and not another" (Job 19:26–27). These lines that smash apart the idols of discord are the recipe for concord, for peace, for the blessed state of the debonair.

In 1940, a refugee from the horrors of the Nazis wrote a letter that was published in *Time* magazine. He said that he had seen the universities collapse before these three egoisms — the self, the state, and the body. He saw the media collapse; the journalists surrender; the courts cave in; and the government institutionalize these roots of discord. Only one voice clearly and serenely spoke out telling the truth, and that was the voice of the Catholic Church. He admitted that he had not thought too much about the Church while growing up, and when he did, he did not think very much of Her. But now he wanted to say that he had a profound respect for the Church as the one voice of peace in a world torn apart.

The man was Albert Einstein. The great scientist was not anti-intellectual, of course, but he once warned that we shouldn't expect intellectuals to show courage in times of crisis. Certainly, there have been great thinkers who have heroically offered their voices, their minds, and their bodies in defense of truth. But collectively, Einstein knew the temptation of pride that haunts the intellectual and that tells us that the ego is god, that our institutions can be god, that our flesh can be god.

We began by discussing the great saint Louis IX, who died on the coast of North Africa at the age of fifty-six. Another great man, Abraham Lincoln—if not a saint, certainly a kind of civil prophet—was fifty-six when he was assassinated. And then, on the other side of the ledger, Adolf Hitler also died at the age of fifty-six. He represents so vividly that image of Samson in the Old Testament bringing the temple of Dagon down upon his head: That's what the dictator did to his own people, to his own nation, and to half the world. This did not have to be: It was the result of human pride, of a compact with the prince of discord.

There was something supernatural, something diabolical, going on in that Nazi bunker. It was a parody of God's gift of life and love and eternal beatitude. Hitler mocked the gift of life by celebrating his own birthday in such macabre conditions. He mocked the charism of love by finally marrying his mistress surrounded by the stench of hatred. And he mocked eternal life by putting a bullet in his own head, declaring himself dictator even over his own soul. "Blessed are the debonair."

But there is also a repudiation of God alive in our world with a destructive force that we can measure right now. We do not have to comb through the warnings of the prophets; all their warnings have come to pass. We see the consequences of the rejection of the voice of God, Who spoke light and peace into the world. We see the consequences of trying to build kingdoms on earth as false utopias. We see the consequences of treating the dignity of man as though it were our own invention, our own plaything, and our own idol.

It is Christ Who gives us peace. It is Christ Who makes the difference between the agents of evil and discord and His saints, the carriers of peace into the world. It is Christ Who says, "Peace I leave with you; my peace I give to you; not as the world gives do I give to you. Let not your hearts be troubled, neither let them be afraid" (John 14:27).

Part 2

Jesus and the Gospels

8

The Crossroads of Life

or

How to Keep Our Eyes on Christ

In New York City years ago, there was a pastor in the Garment District who advertised his church as the "crossroads of the world." (New Yorkers are given to that kind of language.) Well, when he became pastor of a church in Midtown, he advertised *that one* as the "crossroads of the world." This priest was an evangelist and a master of public relations. But he was on to something: Every church is at the crossroads of the world. Indeed, every generation and every civilization finds itself at a crossroads.

But wherever there is a crossroads, there is a cross. When the Cross of Christ appeared in the world, civilization truly was at a crossroads. It would seem that God in His infinite wisdom chose that moment in history precisely because of its drama. Consider that the Crucifixion of Christ happened almost equidistant between the capture of Rome by the general Pompey and the destruction of Rome by the emperor Titus. It was at that crossroads of civilization that the Lord of history made Himself known.

Grace and Truth

At another of the great crossroads in history, the United States Civil War, Abraham Lincoln appeared on the scene. It seems that at certain crossroads, an individual like him appears with no easy explanation—a man who had been defeated time and time again for public office, a man who had been laughed at, a man who did not have outward gifts of charm and success, and yet the right man in the right place at the right time. Abraham Lincoln was self-taught: He learned almost all the humane sciences by reading the Bible and the classics, and through his own experience. In a famous speech in 1858, he quoted Christ. He certainly wasn't the first politician to have done that, but he was a rare politician who understood what Christ meant—specifically that Christ's words at the crossroads of salvation were relevant to the ongoing experience of his country, which was on the road to its own kind of Calvary. Lincoln said to a crowd in his home state of Illinois, "A house divided against itself cannot stand. I believe this government cannot endure permanently, half slave and half free."

He was right about the United States of America. Christ had used this metaphor to describe the human soul, but every nation is a composite of human souls. Just as a nation cannot survive if split between slavery and liberty, neither can a nation survive if the souls of its citizens are half enslaved and half free. Sin is slavery; saving grace is freedom.

The crossroads of every biography is this challenge to the soul: How will we choose? The soul that is governed by what it thinks is freedom but is, in fact, the delusion of pride, falls into slavery. It is pride, the pretense that we can live without the Cross, that splits the soul. The soul is made of the intellect and the will: Passion enslaves the will; pride then co-opts the intellect.

That great voice of the nineteenth century and of all ages, John Henry Newman, spoke to a group of university scholars about pride, knowing that pride is a besetting sin of the intellectual.

He said famously, "Quarry the granite rock with razors. Moor the vessel with a thread of silk. And then you may hope with such keen and delicate instruments as human knowledge and human reason to contend against those giants, the passion and the pride of man."

Passion and pride: This is what Our Lord is speaking of in announcing the hour of darkness. He is describing the prince of lies, who wants us to think that passion — not the Lord's divine and salvific Passion, but our fallen human passion — is the way to freedom, and that pride is the source of our dignity. Our Lord knows that passion and pride can be defeated only by suffering and failure. That's what the Cross teaches us. The Cross has been called the medicine of the world: It is the cure for this deep affliction, this neurosis within the soul that would have us mistake slavery for freedom. When the soul is divided, civilization begins to fall apart.

The consciousness of God is the beginning of accepting the Cross. Once we understand that there is a God, He, by His grace, will show us that He is one, that He is merciful, and that He has the power to draw us unto Him. "I, when I am lifted up from the earth, will draw all men to myself" (John 12:32). Remember the way Our Lord revealed Himself to Moses: "I AM WHO I AM" (Exod. 3:14). He is the source of all life, and indeed of *being* itself.

But if our souls are divided, if our civilization is split apart, we begin to lose the vision of God and His life-giving goodness that had been given to us. God told us, "I AM." And yet, amid the remnants of a broken and decaying civilization governed by passion and pride, instead of proclaiming that God is the great I AM, we are reduced to sniveling observations about truth and eventually gasping out, "*I don't even know what 'is' is!*" Well, as long as we refuse to confront the reality of the great I AM, we will never really know what "is" is. We will never understand the grammar of civilization. We will never grasp the true content of justice.

We don't have to speculate about who this great I AM is: He came into the world in Christ. "I AM the Good Shepherd" (John 10:11). "I AM the Vine" (John 15:5). "I AM the Door" (John 10:9). "I AM the Way and the Truth and the Life" (John 14:6). Here, in this God-man, we find the meaning of our existence, our civilization, our identity.

Our Lord went to the Cross at the crossroads of civilization, and conquered passion and pride through His suffering and His visible failure according to the terms of the world. We have to remember that the suffering of God in Christ was one of the most difficult things for His contemporaries to grasp. It was the mystery that caused many of them to flee the Cross. And even when people did try to identify with the Cross, they often tried to redefine or deny outright the suffering of Christ. These heretical groups within Christianity claimed that Christ was only *pretending* to suffer on the Cross. They could not understand that the divine glory and divine humility were one.

Joseph Goebbels, that vicious propaganda officer of the Nazi machine, wrote in a diary around Christmastime in 1941 that he had just had an impressive meeting with the Führer, who had told him that he very much admired the myth of the pagan god Zeus, the god of all the gods in the Greek pantheon. Why? The Führer explained that he valued Zeus as a figure of benevolence and kindness.

What a difference there is between the smiling Zeus and the pain-wracked, crucified Christ! That's the experience of the twentieth century in a single anecdote. Our civilization suffered through another manifestation of the Gnostic denial of the Incarnation of God. Note especially how, for one of the cruelest men who ever lived, it was easier to choose the sentimental figure of a nonexistent deity than the suffering and failure of Christ on the Cross.

Christ suffered on the Cross to defeat the passion and pride of Satan. And He failed on the Cross. He had to fail — at least according to the lights of a deceived civilization. He had to contradict those criteria for worldly success that animate the passion and the pride of man. Christ cries out on the Cross, "My God! My God, why have You forsaken me?" (see Matt. 27:46). This is not some kind of mythical success story. No mythical god ever cried out like that!

When John Paul Getty was one of the richest men in the world, someone asked him his key to success. He replied, "It's very easy. Rise early. Work hard. And strike oil." (Not very helpful advice really.) Our Lord never said anything like that. Yes, He did rise early; He kept all-night vigils; and He worked hard to the point of sweating blood. But He never said, "Go out and strike oil." Salvation does not depend on luck. "If any man would come after me, let him deny himself and take up his cross and follow me" (Matt. 16:24). We must stand at the crossroads and choose truth over lies, and life over death.

There's an old proverb that goes, "Success is not one of the names of God."[4] These words came from the experience of God's chosen people. When you read those words, you can still hear the lamentations of the Jews in their captivity in Egypt, in their forty years of wandering, in the desolation of their temple, in the Babylonian captivity, in the suffering through the ages, and in the horrors of the twentieth century. The choice between despairing of this world and hope in God's providence is in every life lived at the crossroads.

Christ, the Messiah of the Jews, came into history to show us the resolution between light and dark, between life and death. As

---

[4] Quoted by Cardinal Joseph Ratzinger, Address to Catechists and Religious Teachers (December 12, 2000).

He walked through the crowds on one occasion, He suddenly said, "Who was it that touched me?" (Luke 8:45). One woman of the throng that surrounded Him had touched the hem of His garment, and He knew it. For however many civilizations there are, however many billions of people ever lived, each one of us is known to God when we touch Him.

But we have to call Him by name. We cannot call Him according to our own name, our own concept of what He is or should be. We cannot pretend that He is anything less than the pain-wracked, suffering Christ. Certainly success is not one of His names. When He hung on the Cross and cried out, "My God! My God, why have You forsaken me?" He was saying something that you will not find in any book or saccharine sermon about positive thinking. You will not see it engraved on any smile button. That kind of language is not "Chicken Soup for the Soul." It is, however, the voice of the Lord of history—at the crossroads of history—hanging on the Cross.

"Father, forgive them; for they know not what they do" (Luke 23:34). He is speaking of you and of me and of every man and woman who has walked through the drama of the human experience. "Who touched me?" *I did.* "Well then, who crucified me?" *I did.* If we deny that, then we are governed by passion and pride, and the house of our soul is divided.

Yogi Berra, the master of malapropism, said that when you come to the crossroads of life, "take it." It's not much better advice than that of Mr. Getty, but I think you know what he meant. Christ gives everyone, every day, every time we wake up, a chance to choose. And of all the people who ever lived, we have less excuse than any to make a wrong choice, for we have access to the experience of all the civilizations that have gone before. We have the hard lessons of those who have rejected Christ. We have the consequences of civilizations that have turned their backs on God's beauty and truth and love.

And every soul is offered the perception of the saints, who see at every crossroads the Cross of Christ, Who is the Way, the Truth, and the Life.

9

Galilee and Calvary

or

How to See the Cross in the Sermon on the Mount

"[Jesus] went up on the mountain" (Matt. 5:1). So begins the greatest sermon ever preached. It wasn't much of a mountain by our standards, but it certainly was and is the most beautiful prospect in the Holy Land. Jesus preached the Sermon on the Mount just north of Capernaum, at the northern end of Galilee, looking across its eponymous sea. Really a large lake, the Sea of Galilee reflects the splendid cerulean blue of that sky. To this day, the area is filled with songbirds. It's an idyllic scene.

When I was a child, we used to go up to Bear Mountain on the Hudson River. And along the way in the car, we'd sing a song: "The bear went over the mountain, the bear went over the mountain, to see what he could see. And what do you think he saw? He saw another mountain." When Jesus climbed the Mount of Galilee, He had in His mind's eye another mountain—Calvary. And that's the only way we can truly understand the Sermon on the Mount.

From miles around and from all directions people came to be near Jesus—young and old, rich and poor. They did it for the same reason people throughout the ages have followed philosophers, teachers, and gurus. They may not have put it this way, but they were looking for the key to happiness. They wanted something more than what they had—not a material thing, but a sense, a feeling.

Joy is happiness in the possession of one's good. Unless we have that joy, we're never going to be happy for very long. Happiness as we understand it is merely a feeling, and it can and does fizzle out. That's why people become cynical about keys to enduring happiness. There has never been a teacher in history, other than Christ, who has really presented the key to perfect joy.

In the nineteenth century, a philosopher of logic named Richard Whately said something that may at first seem illogical: "Happiness is no laughing matter."[5] But he's right: Happiness is based on truth, not just a smile on the face. A smile is only an icon, an indication of access to the truth. And if we're made happy by a lie, or if we're made happy only by sensory experience, that smile soon will fade.

Georges Bernanos said that an optimist is a happy idiot, but a pessimist is an unhappy idiot. They are both idiots in the original sense of that word, which is a person focused totally on the self and unable to relate to another. True happiness, however, consists in contact with the Eternal Other, God.

It is an intuition of the human race that happiness becomes a curse if it focuses only on the self. We can see it, for instance, in the Greek myth of Narcissus. Joseph Campbell, a literature professor, wrote popular books in the 1960s on the history of human mythmaking, culminating in a 1988 television series, *The Power of Myth*. He maintained that all religion is a construct of mythical stories meant to guide us to happiness. In so doing, he coined the phrase "Follow your bliss." In his understanding, there is no religion, including Christianity, that is based on authentic historical

---

[5] *Thoughts and Apophthegms* (London: Longmans, Green, 1854).

fact. "True religion" is, for Campbell, an oxymoron. All religious intuition is merely a sublimation of the desire for bliss.

But we know from our own biographies, to say nothing of the collective experience of the twentieth century and all human history, that we can follow our bliss all the way to Heaven—or all the way to Hell. Christianity, we know, is true. It is not just a feeling. It is not a story sublimating the eternal longing for happiness. It is the path to true happiness—the authentic and limitless joy of union with God.

On that day in the ancient Holy Land, Our Lord took the crowd up the mountain and gave them the seven difficult keys to happiness that we call the Beatitudes. When Christ says, "Blessed are …," we can think, "Happy are …" There have been countless wise people throughout history who've sensed some of these keys, but never have they put them together like Jesus Christ—not Aristotle, not Confucius, not the Buddha, not Mahatma Gandhi.

Our Lord speaks especially of "poverty of spirit." He does not mean that poverty is an intrinsic virtue. Poverty is morally indifferent: It can stimulate virtue, or it can corrode it. "Poverty of spirit" really means recognizing that we are worthless without God. A very rich man can have that poverty of spirit, and someone materially impoverished can lack it. And so, too, when Our Lord speaks of hunger and thirst, He is speaking at least in part of the desire for righteousness and for truth itself as revealed to us by God.

When Our Lord finished the sermon, the crowd was filled with admiration and awe. "The crowds were astonished at his teaching, for he taught them as one who had authority, and not as their scribes" (Matt. 7:28–29). The scribes and the Pharisees were lawyers, theologians, and analysts of God's Holy Word. And most of them were good; most of them practiced what they preached. But a great many of them never really understood the meaning and purpose of God's revelation. They had it in their mind, and they taught it to other minds, but it never really penetrated their hearts. But no one spoke with such authority as Jesus, because He was and is the author of all joy.

We said at the beginning that, when Jesus climbed that mount in Galilee, He had another mount in mind. Three years later He climbed a hill outside the wall of Jerusalem—Calvary, from the Latin for "skull." Unlike the Mount of Galilee, it did not look over any lake. It commanded only barrenness and the bare walls of the city. The sky was not blue on Good Friday, but so black that it frightened the people. There were no songbirds, but only the vultures and ravens waiting to pick at the flesh of the Man on the Cross.

From that Cross, Our Lord spoke seven times, and in these words, we find the key to the Sermon on the Mount. Never let anyone reduce the Sermon on the Mount to a list of mortal platitudes. Jesus did not teach us how to stay out of trouble, how to avoid arrest, how to have merely a respectable life in the short span of time we are given on earth. The Sermon on the Mount is the key to eternal happiness.

- The same Lord Who in Galilee had said, "Blessed are the poor in spirit" looks at those at the foot of the Cross and says, "Father, forgive them; for they know not what they do" (Matt. 5:3; Luke 23:34). If they had poverty of spirit, they would realize how rich they could be if only they followed the One Who is dying for them.
- The same Lord Who in Galilee had said, "Blessed are those who mourn" now turns to that young thief on the other cross, the thief who is weeping for a wretched life, and says to him, "Today you will be with me in Paradise" (Matt. 5:4; Luke 23:43).
- The same Lord Who in Galilee had said, "Blessed are those who hunger and thirst for righteousness" now looks

at His Mother, the only one who perfectly hungers and thirsts for God's will, and says, "Mother, behold your son" (Matt. 5:6; John 19:26).

• The same Lord Who in Galilee had said, "Blessed are the merciful" now cries out, "My God! My God, why have You forsaken me?" (see Matt. 5:7; 27:46). He takes on all the sorrows of a merciless world, the only One Who had no reason other than mercy for enduring that deepest psychological desolation.

• The same Lord Who in Galilee had said, "Blessed are the pure in heart" now cries out, "I thirst" (Matt. 5:8; John 19:28). This thirst is not just for pure water; it is for pure souls.

• The same Lord Who in Galilee had said, "Blessed are the peacemakers" now cries out with a voice that splits the veil of the temple, "It is finished" (Matt. 5:9; John 19:30). What is finished is that warfare within the human soul that every person endures. What is finished is that warfare between God and the Antichrist, who brought all sin and death into the world. The victory over sin and death is accomplished.

• And the same Lord Who in Galilee had said, "Blessed are those who suffer for my name's sake," now says from the Cross, "Father, into Your hands I commend my spirit" (see Matt. 5:11; Luke 6:22; 23:46). This is the One Who has resolved the mystery of suffering and pain.

It was over. The Sermon on the Mount had been put into action. It had not passed from the Divine Mind merely into our minds, but from the Divine Mind through the Sacred Heart of Christ into human history, and into the intellect and the will of all those who accept this truth. At three o'clock on that Friday afternoon, no one looked happy. Only Our Lord knew what was about to happen within the next three days. And only Our Lord knew when He preached the Sermon on the Mount what was going to happen in those next three years. And so He was joyful, and He spread joy: Joy is happiness in the possession of one's good, and Our Lord inherits and contains in Himself all that is good.

In that soul-stirring and magnificent scene in Galilee, we see the crowds going up the hill following this one Man whom they trusted, this one Man Who would be able to tell them something more solid than any generation had ever heard before or has ever heard since. When we see that crowd, we see the entire procession of human history — all the generations, all the cultures, all the nations, and, in that motley crowd, each one of us. They asked, "Where did He get all this?" (see Matt. 13:56). And this is the question of every human heart; it is the heart's longing to understand the origin of the Divine Love that is the content of all happiness.

Understanding the Sermon on the Mount means looking at the photo negative of that morning in Galilee and letting it develop over the following three years of Our Lord's ministry. The Sermon on the Mount is not a compilation of platitudes to be printed on a greeting card. The Sermon on the Mount was translated into blood on the Cross. And *that* is the key to all happiness, however strange it may look to the sanitized modern world to see the Cross as the key. This blood washes away all the sadness of the world, not by cleansing us of unhappy feelings, but by radically annihilating the sin and death that are the cause of all the world's sorrow.

The greatest sermon ever preached, the Sermon on the Mount, was preached when Our Lord was only thirty years old. And then at thirty-three He preached from the Cross. Where did He get this wisdom? The rabbis asked this question when He was twelve, and it is on the lips of everyone who takes Jesus seriously. But if we were to live to be one hundred, we would not have the accumulated experience and wisdom to speak the way He did.

For it is not really a matter of where He got the wisdom: The truth is that He is Wisdom. He told His disciples, "He Who has seen me has seen the Father" (John 14:9). He gave us those seven keys to happiness on that bucolic mount north of Galilee, and He gave us the fruition of happiness on the Cross. All of this is summed up in the one blessing He gives the whole human race, "Come, O blessed of my Father, inherit the kingdom prepared for you from the foundation of the world" (Matt. 25:34).

10

Two Men in the Temple

or

How We Prepare Ourselves to Enter God's Home

Jesus spent a lot of time in and around the temple in Jerusalem. When He was twelve, Mary and Joseph took Him there for a coming-of-age ritual, and He famously discoursed with the rabbis, leaving them astonished (and His parents mortified that He had stayed behind after they had left to return home).

Throughout His public ministry He seemed to haunt the porches of the temple. After all, this was His Father's House. The temple was the summation of the longing of the Jews. They would go there singing songs of praise, such as the 122nd Psalm: "I was glad when they said to me, 'Let us go to the house of the Lord!'" These were songs of ascent, chanted by the Jews as they went up the silver steps to be where God was enshrined in the form of the Arc of the Covenant and, after its loss, in the Holy of Holies, a place set apart as a sign that God has not forgotten His people.

The temple featured prominently in Jesus' public ministry, including a famous parable about two men, a publican and a Pharisee. He told this story to people who knew the temple well. "He also told this parable to some who trusted in themselves that they were righteous and despised others" (Luke 18:9). Note that description: the listeners, Pharisees, trusted in their own goodness and then used that self-assurance against others, passing judgment on their souls from afar.

> Two men went up into the temple to pray, one a Pharisee and the other a tax collector. The Pharisee stood and prayed thus with himself, "God, I thank thee that I am not like other men, extortioners, unjust, adulterers, or even like this tax collector. I fast twice a week, I give tithes of all that I get." But the tax collector, standing far off, would not even lift up his eyes to heaven, but beat his breast, saying, "God, be merciful to me a sinner!" I tell you, this man went down to his house justified rather than the other; for every one who exalts himself will be humbled, but he who humbles himself will be exalted. (Luke 18:10–14)

These two men are not so much radically different personality types as they are aspects of each soul. The first man is a sinner—and, of course, we are all sinners—specifically a publican, a man who engaged in secular pursuits with little concern for the law of God. The second man lived well, setting his mind on higher things and learning them inside and out. That is, he was a Pharisee, an expert in the law of God. These two men—probably based on men Jesus saw in His time around the temple—come together in this parable as icons of the heights and the depths of the human soul.

The publican is miserable because he knows he has failed morally. He stands afar off, eyes downcast, begging God's mercy. This is real humility, as opposed to ritual humility. In the Mass, we are supposed to beat our breast when we confess our responsibility for our sins, but the publican really meant it. He knew the depravity

74

of his soul, and so he didn't want to mingle with others, lest they begin to think better of him than he deserved. The word "humility" comes from the Latin *humus*, which means "earth" or "ground." To be humble means to understand that we are mortal.

Humility is not pretending that we are worse than we really are. It is knowing the reality of the fragile condition of the soul. The publican demonstrates this especially by his unwillingness to cast his eyes upward toward heaven: Not only is he convicted of his own guilt, but he knows that there is a splendor that, in his state, would ruin his eyes and, more importantly, shatter his heart.

But he has gone to the temple. He knows that this is the place where all is explained. This publican had faith. The Letter to the Hebrews says that, no matter what we do, works without faith are worthless to God (11:6). Without faith we've missed the whole point; without faith we've lost who we are. Faith is trust in God's plan for the soul, but if we occupy ourselves with busyness, then we simply become consumed with our works.

The second man, the Pharisee, is as righteous as the other man is unrighteous. There's no denying that the publican was a sinner, and a notorious one at that. The sins of which he accused himself were real. The Pharisee, in his way, is also on the mark about himself, at least to the extent that he really was not unjust, or an extortioner, or an adulterer. But then comes the fatal misjudgment: He thinks he is fundamentally better than these sinners. He judges himself by the standard of the man next to him rather than by God's standard. The publican has faith without works, but the Pharisee has works without faith, without trust that God can make him something more than he is. Indeed, he really doesn't want to be more than he is. He is, if you will, a kind of religious utilitarian.

Andrew Carnegie genuinely did a great amount of good with his wealth and power. He was the richest man in the world in his day, but he resolved that he did not want his children to become corrupted, as he had seen happen to so many of the children of Gilded Age plutocrats. He wanted to give all his money away, and he came very close to doing it.

The magnate understood with a steely conscience how to put money to work. Money is indifferent in itself: It can do evil or good, and he did a lot of good with it. But Andrew Carnegie is not on the calendar of saints. He had works, but what we know of his faith is uninspiring. God alone judges him, and we hope that the spirit that moved him to philanthropy, to the love of the brother, eventually moved him to a love of God.

Carnegie had a strange fascination with Herbert Spencer, a contemporary philosopher who asserted that the human experience could be reduced to a scientific formula—specifically an application of Darwin's theory of evolution to the social condition. Following Spencer, Carnegie thought that if people had enough sanitary facilities, sufficient wages, good housing—that is, the material necessities of life—they could reach the fullness of human potential. His model city was Pittsburgh, then notoriously polluted, very grim in every way. He invited Spencer to visit, but after a few days, the philosopher practically ran back to England. He said that he had seen hell; he was not honest enough to say that it was the kind of place he had been calling Heaven.

The turn-of-the-century utilitarian and the Pharisee share a mentality: They both reduce the vision of God to a calculus based on works without faith. The Pharisee was not in awe of God or of the sacred sublimity of the temple of God, as the sinful publican was. He had a proprietary attitude toward it. Indeed, we often come across people who, by virtue of their philanthropy, think that they have a controlling interest in God. They threaten charities or even the Church with canceling their donations if they don't get their way. Works then become leverage, minimizing the dignity of the human soul toward which they should be ordered.

Two Men in the Temple

The sinner, for all his faults, still had an instinct of dignity. He knew that he was a child of God and that he had not met the mark, and so he was afraid to look to Heaven. The Pharisee, however, brazenly looked to Heaven as if he were on the same level with his God. For him, the temple ceased to be the house of God and became the platform for his vanity.

God has given us three keys to living life in His holy place. The House of God is an outward sign of the sanctuary that He has made for Himself and for our souls; we have to get ourselves in order if we're ever going to enter the House of God. The first key is prayer. Both of the men in Our Lord's parable were praying in their own ways, but only the sinner knew that God was really listening. When we perform our daily examination of conscience, we should ask ourselves if we have prayed. If we don't pray, we're like the animals — it's as simple as that. Animals give delight and glory to God in their own natures, but they do not pray. We have a higher calling: We have an imaginative intellect that can reciprocate the Divine Love by our thoughts. And it is in the divine conversation of prayer that we begin to assume the dignity that God desires us to have for all eternity.

The second way we make ourselves suitable inhabitants of God's Holy House is through mortification. This is the death of the senses, a subjugation of our lower passions to our higher reality. If we do not control our passions, our passions will always control us. The publican knew that; he declared himself a victim of his passions. In so doing, he began to mortify his ego, for pride is the fuel that inflames the passions. The Pharisee, on the other hand, was being consumed by pride. He thought he was superior because he had dominion over certain lower passions, but he had succumbed to the deadliest sin of all — the subtle pride of thinking he was safe.

The third key Our Lord gives us is the sanctification of work. The publican did not sanctify his work: He had done his job to make money, and that was it. He had been successful in worldly terms, but he hadn't connected this with the sovereignty of God and his own status as a son of God.

The Pharisee prayed superficially; He did not mortify himself; and, as far as his work was concerned, well, he had done it as well as anyone could, but his standard was still other men. The problem with the Pharisee is not his righteousness, but his self-righteousness. He was so full of himself that he was like the inn in Bethlehem: He had no room for God. This pride reduces us to a kind of ridiculousness. That's the saddest thing about the Pharisee: Grand as he seemed in the eyes of others, he was, simply, silly.

Victor Hugo said that Napoleon, with all his pretensions and boastings and vanities, was an embarrassment to God. That may be the cruelest thing one can say about anyone! If we anger God, well, we still have the potential to become saints. Many saints angered God grievously, but in their humility they beat their breast and were sincere in their sorrow when they called themselves sinners. But to embarrass God means that we have, by our pride, wiped away our potential for holiness.

These two men, the publican and the Pharisee, went into the temple to pray. One man knew he was a sinner; the other did not. Like a man who can't feel pain, he can't resolve the source of what ails him. The sinner did not justify himself simply by calling himself a sinner; he had to put his faith into action. The Pharisee had performed many good acts, but he had to put faith into his acts.

Neither faith alone nor good works alone can save us. The grace of God combines the two, and that is what we call salvation. It is of that salvation that the human race sings when it enters the temple of God, both to weep together and to rejoice together.

11

The Eyes of Christ

or

How Jesus Beckons Us to Follow Him Everyday

At the start of Our Lord's ministry, He looked at fishermen on the Sea of Galilee and said, "Follow me" (Matt. 4:19). They heard His voice, and it was uniquely compelling; they had never heard a voice with such authority. But more than by the voice, they were drawn in by His eyes. That was their first point of contact with Christ, and they would never forget those eyes.

Those men were changed by the eyes of Christ. The life of each one of them ended in a way they could never have imagined: John, homeless on Patmos; Thomas, believed to have died in India; Bartholomew, skinned alive; Andrew, crucified sideways; and Peter, crucified upside down in Rome. And all because of the eyes.

An honest man will look you straight in the eye; a dishonest or superficial man will not. We've all experienced people whose eyes drift away from us as we are talking, usually scanning the room for someone more important to approach. And then there have been people with powerful eyes that reveal deep evil in the soul. Think of the mad monk Rasputin, whose eyes were said to be hypnotic; he became the spark that brought down the Russian empire.

But the eyes of Christ keep looking at the human race and saying, "Get up and follow me." Our Lord healed paralytics, but He did not come into the world only to do that. Every one of His miracles is a sign of His real purpose, which is to lead us to eternity. And so His eyes heal the paralysis of the soul, freeing us for holiness. "Come up! Get up! Put down your nets and follow me," He said to the fishermen. And He says it to us, too, whether our business is fishing or sitting at a computer or doing housework.

The first term for Christianity was simply "the Way." Christians are those who follow Christ, who is the Way. History has been filled with pied pipers whom people have followed, very often to the desolation of their souls. I was once in a hotel elevator with a former secretary of state, a man who had received just about every honor the world has to give. We were both going to the same dinner, but we got off on the wrong floor. He said to me, "I know the way; just follow me." We walked down a hall, and I followed him around the corner. "It's through there," he said, and he confidently opened the door. It was the laundry room.

No human really knows the way as Our Lord does. He has come to energize the soul so that it might have the courage, through the virtues of faith, hope, and love, to follow Him all the way. Time and again, He used parables to explain just how difficult that would be. And the accounts of His three years of public ministry are very clear about this: Most of the people who started to follow Him eventually abandoned Him. It was only when He rose from the dead and sent His Spirit that He was able to empower His people, through the life of grace, to persevere.

Jesus said, "I came to cast fire upon the earth; and would that it were already kindled!" (Luke 12:49). His eyes must have been burning when He spoke those words. That fire is the Holy Spirit, the zeal that cures the paralysis of the mind and the will. Jesus was a man, and He calls us to follow Him in His humanity. John Henry Newman said, "No man is a martyr for a conclusion; no man is a martyr for an opinion. It is faith that makes martyrs."[6] The faith of the Church is trust in the man Who is also God, Who tells us, "I AM the Way, the Truth and the Life."

In His humanity, Jesus looked at the Apostles, and in His divinity, He looks at you and me. Every time we open a newspaper, He's looking at us through the pages we read. Every time we turn on the television, He's looking at us through the scenes we watch. (And He's judging us by what pleases us.) If there are seven billion people in the world, He's looking at us through seven billion eyes. He told us that He is with us in the hungry, in the naked, in the poor, and in the imprisoned. There are the eyes.

Our Lord does not tell us where He intends to lead us: He knows that if we understood the path, we'd fall apart. At the beginning of our lives, we really would not want to know everything that will happen to us. But Our Lord conceals our destiny, not because the tribulations of our earthly life will frighten us, but because our heavenly destiny is simply too glorious for us to bear now. This is why faith is difficult. It is hard to believe—not in any God, but in a *good* God. It is only by following Our Lord that we come to understand the content of goodness. And all of it comes by looking at the eyes.

If we grow in virtue, we will be able to look Him straight in the face. Judas could not: When He betrayed Our Lord, Judas kissed Him on the cheek. That means he was looking over Christ's shoulder, glancing sideways. He could not look Our Lord in the face, and so he went away and destroyed himself. Peter was different. Through he denied Our Lord, three times—three times more than

---

[6] *The Tamworth Reading Room*, no. 6.

Judas! — he was willing to look into His eyes. Peter stood by that fire saying, "I never knew the man," but when they brought Our Lord across the courtyard, hands bound and mouth gagged, Peter's eyes met His, and the Apostle wept. That was the beginning of Peter's conversion back to Christ.

Our Lord bids us to follow Him through three special virtues. First is the virtue of faith, which allows us to trust that He is going to take us to the place He has promised us. That gift of faith requires a total surrender of the soul, not the cowardly surrender to our lower passion, but the heroic surrender of offering all that we have so that He might make what we have and who we are even better. We can never make a half-hearted vow to Christ. If a young couple plan a prenuptial agreement that will divide their goods if their marriage doesn't work, they've missed the whole point of marriage.

God gives us the gift of hope to help us to follow Him — the hope that the place to which we are going will be better than this. Hope is the engine of all progress. There would be no physical science were there not a material hope of discovering something better than what we have now. And so, the soul can only progress and civilization can only progress if there is hope that the look of Christ is the promise of an eternal glory.

And then Our Lord gives us the gift of love, the total surrender of the self for the other. The Apostles began that adventure of love when they dropped their nets to follow Him. To offer the self for the other means that we become great by becoming small. We find ourselves by giving ourselves away.

As the Apostles followed Jesus along the Galilean roads, there was one time when they fell back. As the gap between them and Christ widened, the Apostles suddenly became autonomous and began to discuss which of them was to be the greatest. Our Lord was out of earshot but never out of mind-shot. So, when they arrived at their destination, Our Lord asked them, "What were you discussing on the way?" He knew the answer, and they knew that He knew, and so they did not respond (Mark 9:33–34).

Jesus then took a little child and placed him on His knee, saying, "Unless you turn and become like children, you will never enter the kingdom of heaven" (Matt. 18:3). It is the child who trusts and who follows. Our Lord, Who is a loving God, warns us that if anyone were to harm the least of these little ones, "it would be better for him to have a great millstone fastened round his neck and to be drowned in the depth of the sea" (Matt. 18:6). He's talking about babies; He's talking about the unborn; He's talking about all of us: No matter how old we are, we are His children.

There's an old Spanish proverb: "Tell me with whom you are walking, and I will tell you who you are." All the history books, all the documentaries about the modern experience, and all the philosophical tomes that have tried to analyze the human condition boil down to the economy between a follower and a leader.

I'm sure there were many times when the Apostles got tired and discouraged. Just read the letters of James and John and Peter. In Paul we read about how they all took one essential virtue—love—and made it into a kind of hymn to the Lord. This was the source of energy that kept them going along the road, following the Way. St. Paul says, "It is no longer I who live, but Christ who lives in me" (Gal. 2:20).

Peter, Andrew, James, John, and all of the Apostles saw and experienced things they never expected, including the very best —God Himself—and the very worst—the devil working his way through people and events. The Apostles were human, just like you and me, and they died. And in the last moment, they closed their eyes and then opened them again in another world. We can be certain by the promises of Christ that when they opened them, they saw Christ. And we know that when they looked at Christ, as we shall look at Christ by His grace, the first thing they noticed was not the brow that was lacerated by thorns, or the ears that heard the cries of the crowds along the road, or the mouth that formed a smile when He saw little children coming to Him. No, the first thing they saw was His eyes.

12

Christ Passing By

or

How Everything Depends on Recognizing Christ

I think that when and if, by God's grace, we see Him face-to-face in Heaven, if we may reflect at all upon our earthly lives, we will ask how we ever considered the Holy Mass nothing more than a rote obligation.

St. John Vianney said that if we really understood what happened in the Mass, we would die—not out of fear, but out of love. Christ's Body and Christ's Blood are right there in front of us and within us! It is in part a routine, of course, and there's nothing wrong with that. Breathing is routine, but we die without it. It's when we think it is *only* a routine that we are in trouble. Sometimes we think we've heard the words enough. Sometimes even the Word of God itself, if we're not careful, can bore us. But we never bore God.

The more we understand that Scripture is the words of God, the more we will understand that He is trying to get a message through to us. Sometimes, though, the way the Word of God is preached can give us the impression that it is boring. I get very tired, for instance, of homilists who waste time explaining why Matthew and Mark don't agree on chronology. That's not the point. One distinguished preacher said that only a Scripture scholar who has lost perspective can think that parents dress the children in the morning and lead them to Mass to find out what happened to the Jebusites. God has given us His Word to find out what happened to His Son; He has told us what happened to His Son so that we might understand what He wants to have happen to us.

In every passage of Scripture and in every Eucharistic Sacrifice there is summed up the entire human adventure. We call this "recapitulation": This summing up is seen in every miracle of Our Lord and in every recorded human contact with Him. Our Lord wants us to understand these scriptural accounts as the summary of the big questions we ask about our history, our lives, our very selves. There are no throwaway lines in Scripture. St. John said that if everything Our Lord said were recorded, we could not contain it in all the books in all the world (John 21:25). What we have is what He wants us to have, and for good reasons.

Consider the scene in Jericho, where Our Lord was passing by near that short fellow Zacchaeus. As a tax collector, he was a kind of quisling, a cooperator with a corrupt Roman authority. He was not a friend of His own people, and so he was despised. But he wanted to see Jesus. He knew what others thought of him, but that did not deter him. He was not obsessed with his self-image; he was obsessed with Christ.

Christ is always passing by. Scripture tells us that He passed by a blind man, and the blind man heard the crowd and cried out to Him. Christ was passing by the paralytic, and the people carried the man to Him. The risen Christ was passing by two men on the Emmaus Road, but those two men were so engrossed in their problems that at first they failed to recognize Him.

Christ Passing By

Christ has been passing by throughout human history. Christ was passing by when the Roman Empire fell. Christ was passing by when the Renaissance brought a momentary and blazing golden light to our civilization. Christ was passing by when the explorers crossed the ocean to discover what they thought was a New World. Christ was passing by when our own nation came into being. Christ was passing by when we were conceived. Christ is passing by every day of our lives. He's passing by when we are asleep and when we are awake, when we are at work and when we are at play. He's always there.

Christ was passing by in Jericho, and He saw the diminutive Zacchaeus up on the branch of a tree, legs dangling. Zacchaeus knew he would be mocked, but he climbed the tree anyway. There's a lesson here: By being forgetful of the self, the self sees Christ. And Our Lord saw this funny man out of the corner of His eye. You might say Our Lord was being coy, for He really knew what was in the heart of that man, just as He knew the hearts of everyone in that crowd. Our Lord glanced up, and Zacchaeus looked down at Him. "Make haste and come down," Jesus said, "for I must stay at your house today" (Luke 19:5).

This scene recapitulates every human life. The Christ Who passes by from our conception to our death is always looking for us, and when He sees us make an act of humility, abandoning the self to see Him, He offers to come into our soul. Some lives are much longer than others, but everyone has a chance to invite Christ into the soul. And we do that by making ourselves accessible to Him.

I have a friend who was born in 1907, and I calculated that when he was small, Saint Pius X was pope. Kaiser Wilhelm was ruling the German Empire; Edward VII was ruling the British Empire; Nicholas II was ruling the Russian Empire; and Henry Ford had not yet invented the Model T. This friend lived a long and fruitful life. And yet Christ passes through the life of every child with the same sublimity and significance and consequence as He passes through the long life of an old man.

There is a children's hymn that, like all children's hymns, is really for adults: "Once in Royal David's City." This hymn, written by Cecil Frances Alexander, is usually sung at Christmastime, but it's for the whole year and for all ages. It has this line about the Infant Christ: "For He shareth in our gladness, and He feeleth for our sadness." Think of little children singing that. In a short life, what gladness does a child have? The gladness of finding Mommy on the other side of the door, the gladness of ice cream, the gladness of jumping into a lake. And what sorrow does a child feel? A scraped knee, getting lost in the supermarket. When a child endures a deep sadness, such as a painful sickness or the death of a parent, it seems violently wrong to us.

But the child, no matter how sheltered and protected, eventually will feel sadness and pain and grief, because the child will grow up. Grown-ups know a lot more about those things: the grief of the loss of a spouse, the grief of illness that may even end in death, feelings of depression, failure, and futility. And they also know gladness beyond the grasp of the child: the gladness of success, the gladness of the exchange of vows with a beloved, the deep joy of seeing the world as if for the first time when one goes to a foreign place, and, ultimately, by God's grace, the joy of seeing Him face-to-face.

All this is recapitulated in Christ Himself. We can observe His gladness only when He smiled, but we cannot possibly understand the joy that moved through the Sacred Heart. In those hidden moments, when He must have laughed at those feasts for which He was criticized, we have not the slightest measure of the laughter of the universe that passed through Him. And so, too, when Our Lord wept, we cannot begin to calculate the depth of that sorrow, the weight of those tears. "My God! My God, why have You forsaken

Me?" (see Matt. 27:46). He takes all that on in a recapitulation of the human condition.

He has been passing by this world far longer than we pass through it. Our passage is but the twinkling of an eye, but He made the world! He began to pass through it when He said, "Let there be light," and He will be passing through until the end of time. All this is recapitulated on the Jericho Road. He looked up at Zacchaeus—and Zacchaeus, that little man, is each one of us because we are so very little in proportion to the universe. "Make haste and come down, for I must stay at your house today."

The act of humility that saved Zacchaeus is the same act that saves us every time we open the door of the confessional. We want to see Jesus, and that is where we see Him. He is always passing by, but not seen by most people, in the Holy Mass, which may seem to be a routine unless we open our eyes to Him in the sacrament of Reconciliation. It is only when we invite Him into our souls by confessing our sins that He invites us into His Heart.

"Come down," He says, and we do come down. We come to the very depths of reality when we say, "Bless me, Father, for I have sinned." If it's difficult for us to identify our sins, it's simply because we're not looking closely enough. If only we could see our souls the way He does. It helps to make a good examination of conscience by scrutinizing our souls as thoroughly as we scrutinize what we can discern of others'. We are very good at spotting others' flaws, but that's pride. Humility turns that moral X-ray on our own intellect and will.

When you invite a guest to your home, you take time to prepare the house. If Jesus were to come into your house at this very moment, what would you change? Christ is always knocking at the door, and if we open, He will come in.

Now ask: "What is there in my soul that I would rearrange if I knew He were coming in right now?" And then: "Well, why

haven't I rearranged it already?" Once we begin to do that, especially through the sacrament of Confession, we will hear the voice
of Christ, Who stops and says to you, "Today, right now, I want to
come into your soul."

Part 3

Truth and Civilization

13

The Lever That Moves the World

or

How to Use Our Gifts for the Good of All

Archimedes was born nearly three hundred years before Christ, and he lived for seventy-five years. He used his mind philosophically, mathematically, and for the purpose of invention. He invented several hydraulic pumps; he discovered what we call the law of specific gravity—Archimedes' Principle; he employed what mathematicians call the method of exhaustion to square a parabola, becoming the forerunner of integral calculus. All this he accomplished centuries before the Word was made flesh.

Archimedes lived in the Sicilian city of Syracuse, and he was a patriot. Just as Leonardo da Vinci did in the Renaissance, Archimedes used his mind to design weapons and fortifications to protect his beloved home. When Syracuse was invaded, having done all he could and realizing at the age of seventy-five that he wasn't going to be able to perform physical combat, he just sat in his garden drawing geometrical patterns in the sand, trying to work out another formula. There, he was stabbed in the back.

Grace and Truth

Our Lord calls each one of us to serve Him with our minds and our wills in a specific time and place. He does not want us to deny our humanity, our embeddedness in the natural order. That is, he wants us to use His supernatural gifts naturally. If we live well, we should be able to die well — and to die well means to die naturally, aware of the divine summons, doing what we have always done. The Romans had an old saying, "Do what you are doing." St. John Bosco was edified when he asked a holy child what he would do if the trumpet for the Last Judgment were to sound as he was playing in the schoolyard. With perfect innocence, the child answered, "My Father, I would keep on playing."

This realist attitude finds its fulfillment in what we call the life of grace. When Christ, Who is the bearer of all truth, guides the soul, the soul does not have to contradict humanity. Rather, it transfigures humanity, just as Our Lord was transfigured on the mountaintop. He didn't become something He wasn't. Instead, a light shone *from within*, and Peter and James and John received a glimpse of Heaven on earth. A window is no less a window because light shines through it — indeed, that is its purpose. And so a man is no less human because Christ shines through — indeed, that is our purpose.

Anyone who is good at anything asks a basic question: "Does it work?" Archimedes asked that about his machinery. He eventually became so convinced — and rightly so — about the power of levers from his experiments that he said, "If you give me a lever big enough, I can move the world." He knew that there was no such lever, of course, but he also knew that, in theory, it could work. It is the same with our human nature. We know our limits, but God also tells us that with the assistance of His grace, our nature can do things beyond its natural capacity without contradicting its natural reality. Sanctifying grace bestows this supernatural potential — the potential of the perfection and elevation of our nature.

A saint is simply a human who is more human than nature on its own would permit.

At the very heart of the Catholic vision of grace is a philosophical principle: There is nothing in the intellect that is not first in the senses. There is a stunning realism in this. It contradicts the fantasies of philosophies that deny God: If you deny God, you really are denying the world. And if you deny the world, you have to redefine the world according to your own fantasy. One of the principal fantasies we indulge is that the world is just an accident.

If you asked Archimedes if he agreed that only reality is real, he would look at you blankly. "What else could be real," he would say, "but reality?" This is a commonsense attitude, and it motivates the best physicists — and the best theologians. But common sense is quite uncommon in our time, for civilization is at a crossroads. It may very well be disappearing.

I do not mean to sound hopeless when I say that. Hope is a virtue, and despair a vice. But I do not countenance the kind of false optimism that can be a pagan substitute for hope. We are not called to hope against hope; we are called to hope *with* hope. And the beginning of hope is to acknowledge reality. The only way to rebuild society is to recognize that it has fallen.

One of the components of the collapse of what we have known as Western civilization is the denial of reality. For instance, some forms of what is called political liberalism denied the reality of Original Sin. Many of the first Enlightenment liberals believed the myth of inevitable progress. But even as liberal civilization fell into that myth, it was living off the Christian truth that there is a kind of progress. God showed that to the world through the history of the Jews, when they progressed from bondage into freedom. But progress requires toil, and so the Jews spent forty years in the wilderness. We can progress from tyranny to freedom only through such toil.

Grace and Truth

When Jesus walked on water, the men in the boat lapsed into a kind of modernist theology. They said it couldn't be so. They saw what Jesus did, but their mind could not explain it, and so they rejected it. In fact, they shouted, "It is a ghost!" (Matt. 14:26). And so when Our Lord rose from the dead, He deliberately returned with His wounds, and He, with magnificent deliberation, asked for something to eat. He knew that the world's response would be, "It can't be. It must be a ghost." And so He replies, "A spirit has not flesh and bones as you see that I have" (Luke 24:39).

Now, Archimedes made a big claim about the power of levers. But he also said that, in order to move the world, he needed a place solid enough to hinge the lever. It is Christ Who moves the world, and the place He chose to do it — the fulcrum of the world — was Calvary, the rock shaped like a skull, that little hill of execution outside the walls of Jerusalem. What could be more real than a skull, the *memento mori*. Ancient philosophers used to put skulls on their desks to remind them of their mortality. They knew that one of the dangers of the abstract intellect was imagining a world in which we might forget that we are natural beings.

If we're going to focus on reality, we need to get back to that question "Does it work?" Does Christianity work? Well, here are two pieces of evidence.

The saints. If you have the misfortune of arguing about religion, you will find yourself discussing doctrines, Church history, and the ups and downs of religious experience. But the one subject artfully avoided by the enemies of reality is the saints. The saints are living proof of how grace does not destroy nature but perfects it.

Without grace, you cannot explain a saint. They are not people who are simply motivated by an exceptional interest in doing good. They are not people who just happen to have an extraordinarily high IQ. They are not people who manage to be at the right place at the right time. And they are not people who are able to manipulate crowds only by attractive personalities. Those excuses will not suffice to explain the saints.

When St. Paul was still known as Paul of Tarsus, he had a highly trained mind and a degree of political influence. It was only after his conversion on the Damascus road, though, when he could cry out, "It is no longer I who live, but Christ who lives in me" (Gal. 2:20), that he became ever more vividly Paul the saint. He did not become less of a man because of Christ; he became more of a man.

The denial of God and His grace — and therefore the denial of the reality of the saints — is at the root of all fantasy. To deny grace is to deny God's access to the soul. It would be very foolish indeed to say that a window is a window only at night. A window becomes ever more a window when the light shines through it. Well, that's the principal of grace; that's realism. The saints are powerful evidence that Christ works in history.

Civilization. We take civilization for granted. It seems to have always been. But civilization reached its greatest heights when minds and wills tried to stretch upward to God, literally thrusting buildings up as if they were trying to touch Heaven. We live in a time in which civilization is crumbling. It is a simple fact that many of our institutions and our general perception of the moral order and our willingness to promote and defend human dignity are disintegrating. One reason this is happening so quickly is that people have become so accustomed to civilization that it is hard for them to believe that it can possibly collapse. Moreover, people with good intentions often don't suspect or understand the power of evil. The last century is an open textbook giving us instructions in the power of evil over unsuspecting people. The most civilized nations in the world in the twentieth century succumbed to the most lurid barbarities, all because people thought that civilization is self-perpetuating.

Grace and Truth

One of myths of the naïve soul is that progress is inevitable. This is, fundamentally, a denial of Original Sin. But even as it fantasizes that truth away, our modern world uses language given by God. We can speak of progress at all only because the world is designed according to an order. There is a goal to life. There is a purpose for creation. When the Jews came out of bondage in Egypt into freedom in the land of promise, God was showing us the course of history. Christianity is not a theory. It is a fact. It is not a wishful thought. It is reality. Therefore, we say it is a historical religion. Indeed, it is what comes at the end of all religion. It is what all religion has sought to achieve.

The grace of God calls each of us in a unique way to serve Him in a particular time and place—so that we might be with Him forever. To manifest His creative harmony, He calls upon us to be living proofs of His grace as saints—first, by living the life of holiness and, second, by transfiguring culture. Slavery was abolished because of the Christian vision, because of Christians who finally said, "This must stop." Christian philanthropy, one century after another, has been promoted by, and in turn has promoted, the vision of human dignity endowed by God. The early Christian monk Didymus the Blind—a teacher of St. Jerome who called him Didymus the Seer—started a foundation to care for the indigent blind. In modern times, another Catholic designed and gave his name to Braille. In the nineteenth century, the Abbé le Pey, a French priest, developed sign language.

I mention these examples in particular as evidence that it is the Church Who wants people, whether hindered by moral or physical blindness, to see reality. Our Lord knows, though, that physical blindness does not impede our way to Heaven, but moral blindness does. In the early years of the Church, a Christian woman named Fabiola endowed what probably was the first hospital in civilization. In our own day, the Mayo Clinic was at first staffed by Catholic nuns. The grace of God transforms the world through science. It was the Christian vision of the goodness and order of creation that promoted what we call the scientific method.

In arts and in literature, the Catholic voice has manifested to the world the right use of the mind and of matter: for the glory of God. Cézanne and Bernini, two artists, very dissimilar in style, went to Mass every day recognizing the sacred vocation God had given them with paintbrush and chisel. And in more modern times, we can look to the music of Palestrina, Monteverdi, Vivaldi, Corelli, Haydn, Mozart, Bach, Beethoven, Bruckner, and so on.

Just as a saint cannot be explained without the grace of God, neither can these high achievements of civilization. And even if the artist, even if the musician, even if the scientist does not fully articulate or explicitly acknowledge the source of his inspiration, it is still there. And the more one lives the life of grace, the more invention and art and science literally becomes full of grace.

"If you give me a lever big enough, I can move the world." Well, that lever does exist. That lever is the Cross. And it would be the ultimate denial of reality to say that Jesus did not move the world when He hung on that Cross. He is the beginning and the end. And His grace moves saints in every age, and it continues to do so in our day in ways that we do not yet perceive, but will know generations from now, as He moves the world all the way to Heaven.

14

Art and Laughter

or

How Beauty and Mirth Orient Us to God

"For the law was given through Moses; grace and truth came through Jesus Christ" (John 1:17). The law is the ordering principle of the world: In the natural order, we speak of natural law, and in the soul we speak of the moral law. But this law is empowered by God's presence: His grace and His truth.

When the soul is full of grace and truth, it sings. This is an instinct of the human condition: When we are happy, we sing; and when we are sad, we sing. One kind of song praises order, and the other mourns the collapse of an order. Harmonious music is heavenly laughter come to earth. When Our Lord was born, the heavens opened, and a great joy was heard as the angels sang, "Peace among men with whom he is pleased!" (Luke 2:14). In other words, it is only the soul in harmony with God that can understand the song of Heaven.

Laughter is a moral reality; we can tell this by the fact that it can be either pleasant or unsettling. When people laugh at something that is genuinely funny, in a good spirit, it truly is medicine for the soul. But we are horrified by the sound of people laughing at what is evil, disordered, and obscene.

It is said—by whom I cannot say—that the average child laughs 113 times a day while the average adult laughs only 11 times. Whatever we make of the numbers, we can understand the principle: Children laugh a lot more than grown-ups. Something happens in the process of growing up, as the years take their toll, that diminishes laughter—and we should not call it "maturity." Only God's grace can restore that laughter.

Without holy laughter, indeed, we are not human. This isn't just my idea: Thomas Aquinas said that one definition of a human being is the ability to laugh. Risibility is a quality animals cannot have. We are projecting the gift of laughter onto lower creatures when we think they are laughing in the way we do. For sure, they delight in God in their own ways, and God delights in them. But we, through the harmony of intellect and will, are able to laugh, to perceive order and the incongruity of disorder.

G. K. Chesterton said, "Almost without exception the greatest philanthropists in the world lack two things: laughter and humility." He was very suspicious of millionaires. The philanthropist, with all his good works, is not pleasing to God (or really to man) unless he can also spread God's grace and God's truth. Andrew Carnegie, the most famous magnate in the world in Chesterton's time, drove the writer almost to distraction. He said, "Andrew Carnegie is a good man, but he could be so much more if only someone were to roll him in a barrel down the street."[7] Laughter and humility are the two things lacking in secular humanism. Laughter is a gift and manifestation of grace. Humility is a gift and manifestation of truth.

[7] *Illustrated London News*, December 29, 1906.

Just as it is in our better nature to sing, so it is in our better nature to arrange words in poetry. In the late seventeenth century in Southampton, England, there was a boy who was addicted to verse. As a boy, Isaac Watts watched a mouse by the fireplace and said, "The little mouse, for want of stairs, went up a rope to say his prayers." His father told him to cut it out. The family had had enough of his constant scansion. He replied, "Father, father, pity take, and I will no more verses make." He didn't keep his poetic promise. Instead, he became the father of English hymnody, writing hundreds upon hundreds of church songs. We still sing many of them: "Joy to the World," "O God, Our Help in Ages Past," "When I Survey the Wondrous Cross."

Watts did not compose the music to his lyrics, but music is an essential, complementary part of hymnody. Like grace and truth, music and words go together. When we take the best music and the most truthful words and combine them and offer them to God, then we have sacred music.

The twentieth-century Swiss theologian Hans Urs von Balthasar wrote much about music and all the mysteries of beauty in God's creation. He was a good friend of the Calvinist theologian Karl Barth. While they didn't agree on all religious doctrines, they did agree about Mozart; in fact, they regularly got together to listen to his music. Balthasar had one of the most phenomenal minds of the modern age. He memorized Mozart's corpus so thoroughly that he threw out his Victrola turntable and listened to whatever he wanted in his head, playing it in his mind. It was extraordinary. He once said rather whimsically that he supposed that the angels play Bach when they are performing for God — but amongst themselves, they sing Mozart.

Tastes can vary, it is true, but it is only the barbarian who says that all taste is subjective. There is a hierarchy of standards for the good, the true, and the beautiful. If we do not conform ourselves to

God as the source of these things, then we lose that triad. The good becomes mere sentimentality. The truth becomes mere pedantry. The beautiful becomes mere aestheticism.

The Church raises our artistic capacity for making harmony and expressing truth to its highest at the Eucharistic Sacrifice of the altar—the central moment of civilization. It is here that the angels and the saints gather together, singing the truth of God come to earth. The Second Vatican Council said that, at the Mass, the song of the Heavenly Jerusalem comes into our midst.

The Church does not promote music out of a vain aestheticism. Rather, it is because grace and truth have come to us through Christ, and that means that we sing. And we sing not only nice-sounding music; we sing words of truth. The music must serve the words. For this reason, the Church has given pride of place to Gregorian chant, because with its mathematical symmetry, the music never overwhelms the meaning. The sentimentalist lets music run away with the soul without obeying the words. But the more the vision of Heaven becomes palpable, the nobler both the music and the verse become.

At the end of the first millennium, there was a pope who was an accomplished musician as well as a theologian: Sylvester II. Some of his critics, trying to explain his brilliance, said he must have sold his soul to the devil. He was a renaissance man before the Renaissance: Among other accomplishments, he helped develop modern water piping. But more importantly he wrote sacred verse to be sung. Everything he wrote, though it had to follow the laws of meter and rhyme, conformed to the truth of the gospel.

Cardinal Newman, in the nineteenth century, spoke about the development of doctrine, giving certain principles by which we can analyze and understand how Church doctrine is legitimately re-expressed from age to age in new language, but always consistent to its essential integrity. One of the criteria for authentic development of doctrine was what he called a "continuity of type." In other words, the essential message is never changed. I can change the language in which I say it; I can alter the imagery that I use to express it; but the fundamental principle never changes.

In the Counter-Reformation, one of the most exuberant periods of Catholic artistic life, Giovanni Palestrina promoted a system of intricate harmonies and descants that we call polyphony. Pope Marcellus finally assented to this, but he insisted that there be a *cantos firmas*, a consistent melody, which the harmonies may decorate but which remains consistent, audible, and predominate. In so doing, he gave us a musical model of what Newman meant by the continuity of type. All great music is harmonious. It does not promote discord or evil passions. It has symmetry. It has a goal.

Our friend Chesterton said that "Jazz was the song of the treadmill." That may have been something of an arbitrary expression of taste, but he was expressing the essential principle that great music must have a goal; it must attain a finale. Plato banned from his ideal republic "corybantic" music, which was music that, through the use of repetitious drumbeats and nonsensical words, deliberately dimmed the intellect and inflamed the lower passions. Who could deny that popular music today is defined by precisely those aims? We need not commit ourselves to any arbitrary expression of taste to say that Catholics must be committed to the exhibition and manifestation of grace in truth through the forms of art accessible to us.

Pope Benedict XVI, in his wonderful writing on music, said that we must begin with the Gloria of the angels at the Incarnation, that celestial laughter that cheered the cold, neglected stable. He points out that in the traditional Mass, the Canon (the Eucharistic Prayer) was said silently as the Sanctus (the "Holy, Holy, Holy") was sung. This was because this celestial music of the cherubim accompanies, on the part of the gathered Church, the voice of the priest offering, in the name of Christ, the perfect sacrifice of the Body and Blood.

With the choir and the clergy and the congregation all doing their part, they form a greater harmony, a kind of collective liturgical polyphony. We have to wash out of our minds a lot of the more recent liturgical nonsense we've been fed. We have been afflicted with some of the most banal, brutal, ugly, destructive, and vicious substitutes for sacred music in our generation. Nevertheless, there endures that essential vision that motivates all the saints, the vision of the celestial laughter of Heaven come into our midst.

In the practical order, then, with the same sensibility that motivated Plato to ban corybanticism from the ideal republic, it is the tradition of the Church to discourage the use of percussion instruments, since percussion amplifies the rhythm of the untransfigured passions. Rather, the strings and the wind instruments, including and especially the organ, are appropriate to the Liturgy. Since all the music is part of a gathered offering to God, it is inappropriate for the singers to face the faithful. The faithful are the essential singers; therefore, it is far more fitting that the choir be disbursed amongst the people and, ideally, in a loft behind the people, for theological and acoustical reasons. A confrontation between the leader of song and the people sends the wrong message about the relationship between the music and the people. These practical matters aside, and some of them can be disputed, there abides the fact that, in order to make worthy music for the courts of Heaven, we need laughter, and we need humility. It's not banal laughter that we need, sometimes expressed in the form of false informality and even applause in church. On the contrary, in the sacred space, the divine laughter must bring us to a reverent and solemn silence. And so, too, if we are humble, we will not congratulate or entertain ourselves in church.

We will offer the song of the angels and nothing less.

Art and Laughter, or How Beauty and Mirth Orient Us to God

John Henry Newman, in addition to being one of the great theologians of Catholic history, was an accomplished violinist. Even at an advanced age, his most prized gift was a violin that he played until his fingers became too arthritic to go on. In one of his sermons, he said, in words that are a sacred song themselves:

> Is it possible that that inexhaustible evolution and disposition of notes so rich, yet so simple, so intimate and yet so regulated, so various, yet so majestic, should be a mere sound which is gone and perishes? It is not so. It cannot be. No, they have emerged from some higher sphere. They are the outpourings of eternal harmony in the medium of created sound. They are echoes from home.
>
> They are the voice of angels or the Magnificat of saints or the living law of divine governments or the divine attributes. Something are they beyond themselves which we cannot compass, which we cannot utter, though mortal man, and he perhaps not otherwise distinguished above his fellows, have the gift of eliciting them.[8]

---

[8] *Letters and Diaries*, vol. XXII, p. 9.

15

Maternal Memories

or

How the Church Keeps the Human Tradition Alive

Some friends once took me to visit a nursing home run by the Little Sisters of the Poor, who do magnificent work with the elderly in their last years, preparing them for the glory of God. The sisters act not simply as providers of medical assistance but as citizens of God getting ready for the Eternal Kingdom. There is something about a home for the elderly run by people who believe in eternal life that transfigures the trials and the infirmities of old age.

That was apparent in this nursing home, especially with one woman who was over one hundred years old. She was incredibly lucid as she began to tell me about going to California from St. Louis in a covered wagon when she was a girl. As she told me this story, I realized that I was hearing one of the last firsthand accounts of that era in our nation's history that opened literally an entirely new world to our civilization. They traveled by night, she said, because it was cooler then and also to avoid attacks from Indians. It was chilling, in a wonderful way, to hear this from someone who had been through it. She had lived more than a century, and she had a long memory.

But, in the perspective of eternity, even this woman's memory encompasses but a tiny period of history. And so, we need a chain of memory, a chain that is usually formed by the teaching of mothers, who pass down the lore of the tribe. Of course, men have memories too, but in my experience, men are more reluctant to talk about the tribe, about the ancestors, than women are. The woman is the guardian of the hearth, as in Roman days, when the vestals kept the flame that was the sign of the heart of Rome.

Once a woman told me her father had spoken with Abraham Lincoln. He knew Lincoln to some small degree, and in those days, one could just wait in the White House to see the president without much formality. And I asked her what her father said Lincoln was like. She responded, "Oh, I was very small then, and I don't remember very much. Papa always spoke very highly of Mr. Lincoln." I once lived in a small town in New England where a woman boasted that her mother had sat on the knee of Daniel Webster. And in another nursing home, a woman told me that when she was a student at Wellesley College, she had a teacher, Katharine Lee Bates, who wrote poetry. At the start of one school year, Miss Bates told them a little of her vacation out West, took out a piece of paper, and read to them a new poem of her composition, "O beautiful for spacious skies, for amber waves of grain ..."

I once heard a story of an old man who said to a young friend, "Young man, give me your hand." And when the little boy did, the old man said, "When you are an old man, you will be able to tell your grandchildren that you shook the hand of a man who shook the hand of a man who shook the hand of George Washington." Washington didn't shake many hands: When he was president, he kept his hands behind his back and bowed, a gesture he thought was proper to the dignity of this new office.

The story is one of a kind of civil apostolic succession, passing on the *memory* of a *fact*.

We have an imagination that can invent symbols, signs, and fictitious characters, but the memory recalls real people who did real things. The Church is apostolic: That means She carries the memory of a fact—the fact of Jesus Christ. And that fact is not recalled nostalgically, but it is passed on personally. Our Lord gave the power and the commandment to His Apostles to preach the gospel, to be the gospel, to be Christ. That is why traditionally the bishop, who is a successor of the Apostles, wore a plain cross rather than a crucifix, because he represents the living memory of Christ to the people.

By God's grace, memory confers youth. One has to be old to have a long memory, but that memory changes the weakness of age into strength. This is why the saints seem to get younger as they get older: They grow older biologically, but they grow younger spiritually. A friend of mine had a mother in her nineties who was overheard by a nurse shortly before she died saying into a mirror, "Is it not wonderful how something so old can be so beautiful?" Remember the Song of Solomon, "Arise, my love, my fair one, and come away; for lo, the winter is past, the rain is over and gone" (Song of Sol. 2:10–11). This is the voice that Our Lord speaks to the oldest people as they are dying: "My love, my fair one, arise and come away."

Shortly before my mother died, I said something to her that she properly disagreed with. She said, "Remember, no matter how old you are, I am still your mother!" To which I pompously replied, "Our Lord once said, 'Who is my mother?'" And she replied in turn, "Well, if He said it, I'm sure He did not use that tone of voice!" She was right! Think of how Our Lord must have spoken to His Mother. In the temple at the age of twelve, He seems to speak in a severe tone: "Did you not know that I must be in my Father's house?" (Luke 2:49). But there was a connection between their eyes and their hearts, for when He said "my Father's house," she knew what He meant: She knew what the temple was, and she knew Who His true Father was.

Similarly, at the wedding at Cana, Our Lord seems to be sharp and unfeeling when He says, "O woman, what have you to do with me? My hour has not yet come" (John 2:4). But she knew, as He knew, why He used such an impersonal address: She is the New Eve. She is the prototype of what the human race is supposed to be when we do the will of God. From the Cross, again, He said, "Woman," for she, the New Eve, was participating in the repair of the breach between God and man that went back beyond memory to our first ancestors (John 19:26). The only inkling that we have in the human memory of the Fall of man is the inchoate recollection that there had been a Paradise—and it was shattered.

Then and today and until the end of time, the Church passes on the memories of the tribe—the tribe of Christ. The Church is not an "it." The Church is our Mother. She is the guardian of culture, and where the Mother is loved, there is a culture of life. When the Mother is scorned, we inherit a culture of death. When Pope John Paul II said that we are living in the culture of death, he meant that we have lost our memory of the human drama, of the combat between good and evil, and of the promise of grace.

At the heart of a culture of life is the memorial of the Mass —Holy Mother Church's Sacred Meal. The Church has a memory that is not nostalgic but efficacious; She passes on the *fact* of the Eucharistic Meal, not a passive recollection of a one-time past event. The Church animates the Passover so that it becomes the presence of Christ, Who leads us from the bondage of sin into the Promised Land. "Do this in memory of me," we hear, but the original word really means something far more subtle than our translation can easily capture. *Anamnesia* means recovering one's memory, not merely in the sense of recollecting what had been lost in the mind, but of bringing back into reality that which did exist but which we had forgotten. The memorial of the Mass does not just rivet our minds on the Christ of two thousand years ago; it passes Him on to us.

Mothers have a very long memory, and Holy Mother Church has the longest memory, for She knows that there was a Paradise. She knows that there was a first man and a first woman created by the gratuitous love of God. And She knows everything that happened along the way until this day.

Socrates used to look at newborn babies and marvel at how old they looked, for really there is nothing that looks more like an old man than a little boy who has just come out of his mother's womb—hairless, toothless, fragile. Socrates surmised from this that each baby had a previous, long life, and the process of birth was the blocking of the memory of that life. Education, he proposed, would consist in recovering the memory, just as a midwife brings life out of the womb. His method of teaching was called the midwife method.

Of course, Socrates was wrong about that preexisting intelligence. But, analogically, he was onto something: By the fact of our very existence, we have inherited a life larger than our own: the life of culture. Our Lord says that He must leave this world in order to send us the Holy Spirit, Who will lead us into all truth. The Holy Spirit opens our memory through the virtues of faith, hope, and love, and through those particular gifts of prudence, justice, temperance, and fortitude, by which we put the memory to work.

We have to give thanks that in the midst of the culture of death there is life. And that life is found in the Holy Catholic Church. "With His own blood He bought Her," says the hymn. The Church is our Mother, and She confers upon us the dignity of sons and daughters of an ancient ancestral procession. If we forget that, we can recover the memory through the life of grace. There's nothing so dead as a grown man or woman who has forgotten the past. This is how civilization gets lost. The only way to find the way out of the woods is to remember how you got there.

The Old Testament prophets did that, but they were only pointing to the Source of all memory, Christ Himself. He comes into the world and says, "Before Abraham was, I am" (John 8:58). That's not bad grammar. It would be for us, since we are not divine. For Jesus, though, it means that He started it all. And all those sages, seers, and prophets who have become part of the collective memory of the Church were sent by Him to waken us up to the fact that there is a life and that it is passed on through the Church, as a mother passes on life through her womb.

Remember the man who shook the hand of the man who shook the hand of the man who shook the hand of George Washington? Well, we can do better than that. We don't have to *think* back to Christ: He passes Himself on, hand laid upon head, hand laid upon head, to one bishop after another. Their job is not simply to talk about the Christ Who *was*. The gospel they are anointed to preach is the Good News that Christ is alive *today*.

A human mother knows the temptations that will beset her child, and if she lives long enough, she can observe and nurture that child, physically and morally, as he grows into maturity. But the Church in Her supernatural maternal character knows the temptations of all stages of life, from infancy to the grave. And so She warns us that in youth we'll be tempted especially by lust, in middle age especially by the thirst for power and control, and in old age by that most insulting affliction of all—Satan's last chance to grab us—and that is greed. For greed is the weak and feeble human attempt to fabricate eternal life. The maternal memory of the Church knows how illusory all of these deceits are.

There is a lovely painting by the Spanish artist Francisco de Zurbarán showing the Blessed Mother as a young girl seated on a chair. On her lap is some embroidery she's working on, but when you look carefully, you realize it's the shroud of her Son. This image prefigures the role of the Mother from the very moment of Christ's conception.

We are born to live. He is born to die and to rise again that we might live forever. And the only reason we know that is because the Church is not an "it." She's our Mother, the Mother with the longest memory.

16

National Tragedy

or

How Hard Times and Evil Men
Highlight Forgotten Truths

In 1789, on Wall Street, George Washington was inaugurated the first president of the United States. Afterward, he went to St. Paul's church down the street, and he prayed. The church is still there, along with its cemetery, with graves hundreds of years old. On September 11, 2001, in the haste of terror, fresh corpses were laid on top of those graves. When the first tower came down, there was running and there was screaming. But when the second tower came down, there was only a massive groan. It seemed that the weight of the world itself was coming down, and people just sat on the ground. They didn't run anymore; they just sat and groaned.

When reporters asked witnesses to describe the scene, I think of lines from the sixth book of Virgil's *Aeneid*, when Dido asks Aeneas to describe the wreck of his ships and the drowning of his men: "Oh, Queen, you asked me to tell a tale that should not be uttered."

September 11 destroyed not only buildings but three lies that we have been told for far too long. The first lie is that there is no natural law. We've had at least an entire generation that has been told that nature is an accident and that the will of God expressed in the harmony of creation is a fluke. We've been told that laws passed by Congress and decisions of the Supreme Court owe no allegiance to the natural law, and even that they may alter it. But we saw on September 11 the natural law at work.

The natural law is enshrined in the American civil experience in those famous rights articulated in the Declaration of Independence: life, liberty, and the pursuit of happiness. Happiness, properly understood, is the goal of the human condition. Ultimate happiness means being happy with God, but we have a choice of accepting God or rejecting Him. The ability to make that choice is supported by ordered liberty. And liberty can be exercised, of course, only if we're alive. And so, the fundamental natural right is that to life.

In our culture of death there are those who say there is no right to life — that life is not granted by God, that life is really just a decision of other people exercising their idiosyncratic wills. We can decide who should live and who should die. That was shown to be false — by the actions of the very people steeped in these lies — on September 11.

As people ran away from the carnage and the smoke and the collapsing buildings, I saw a young couple running with a baby carriage. There is an instinct in the human condition to preserve the little ones, to defend the innocent. The more civilized we are, the more we let that instinct flourish — but the barbarians would destroy it. According to the logic of our culture, and according to certain expert philosophical theories, that young mother and father would have been perfectly free to abandon their child to save their own necks. But they didn't.

One young man was opening his front door on his way to work when his wife cried out: She was going into labor. Instead of going to his office, which was in Tower One, he rushed her to the hospital. As the baby emerged from the womb of his mother, the tower collapsed. The first thing that that little baby did was to save his father's life. This destroys the lie that life is merely a burden. All life is a gift, and the right to life is guaranteed to us by God — and all civilized laws recognize that. Life is given to us by God as a sign of hope; to reject its goodness is to despair.

The second lie that was put to rest, at least temporarily, on September 11 is the lie against the priesthood. Many historians have remarked that the hatred of priests is as old as the human rebellion against civilization. There is an intrinsic connection between the priest and the eternal truths that the anarchist would destroy. Certainly the clergy through history has been justifiably criticized and has been subject to legitimate reforms. But the priesthood of the Catholic Church was instituted by Christ. He is the High Priest, and all priests work in His Name — and they are especially accountable for how they go about that.

Furthermore, there can be a Eucharist, which is a Sacrifice, only if there is a priest. Attacks have been made on the priesthood from outside the Church, but also from within the Church, by those who are repulsed by the idea of sacrifice. But on September 11, we saw the sacrificial priesthood. We saw blood. I saw one priest who had been killed and carried into St. Peter's Church on Barclay Street. He was killed only because he volunteered to be on the scene giving the last rites of the Church. His body was laid in front of the altar.

In St. Peter's, there is behind the altar an oil painting of the Crucifixion of Christ, of Christ bleeding from the Cross. The fire chaplain's body was reverently laid in front of the altar covered with a sheet, but blood still flowed from the body down the sanctuary steps and into the aisle. This was an icon of the priesthood — real blood, a real priest, a real altar — and all because of Christ on the Cross. A generation that has been told that sacrifice is self-destructive began to see on that day what real destruction is — and where the real source of life is: the offering of the self for the other. "Greater love has no man than this, that a man lay down his life for his friends" (John 15:13).

The third lie that was destroyed on September 11 was the lie whispered throughout human history by the prince of lies: that there is no truth. We have, as a people, stopped saying "I think" or "I know" and say instead "I feel." Pope St. John Paul II issued encyclicals about the loss of belief in objective truth, which he marked as the central crisis of our age. Pius XII said that the great sin of the modern age was a loss of a sense of sin itself. This is true as well, but the abandonment of the idea of truth is really just the obverse of that. For it is only when we know what is truth and what is falsehood that we can know what is sin and what is virtue.

On September 11, policemen and firemen came to priests to be absolved of sin. And even as metal was falling, they would take their helmets off for blessings. There were so many that eventually the priests were giving general absolution the way one does on a battlefield—and this was a battlefield. Seeing that scene, smelling the acrid smoke—which was not just chemical smoke, but the smoke of burning flesh redolent of all the acrid smoke of the modern age, which has consumed men and women, body and soul—the priest was able to say in the Name of Christ, "I absolve you from your sins, in the Name of the Father and of the Son and of the Holy Spirit."

Those rescue workers were not going through a formality. They knew what they were getting into, and they knew how to get out of it—not how to get out of earthly death, but how to get out of eternal death. One can ask for absolution only if one knows that there is a True God Who will absolve sin. One can only speak of sin if one knows virtue. And one can know virtue only if one knows the ultimate truth that there is a God in Whose image we are made. In other words, we have an intellect and a will that can reflect the offering of God, Who, in a gratuitous act, said, "Let there be life." All virtue is a participation in that life.

In one of the subway stations, smoke was blinding people as they tried to work their way up the stairs to fresh air. They had no idea what was going on at first, and they panicked because they were temporarily blinded by the harsh smoke. One man raised his voice to them to calm down. He took each one of them by the hand and led them up the stairs to safety, by a route only he knew — more precisely, a route only he and his seeing-eye dog knew. Day in and day out, these commuters had seen that man and pitied him for his blindness. But in that crisis, he was the only one who could see.

It reminded me of how many times in the history of the saints that people had pitied them for some reason or another, thinking that they had missed out on the joy of life or had denied themselves too many pleasures, only to find out in the end that the saints were the only ones who could really see. It may be that September 11 was a wake-up call. But if we awake in the morning, we have to get out of bed. And once we are out of bed, we have to go to work. And if we're going to work as humans in the image of God, instead of as drones and slaves, we have to know that God has ordained a plan for the human soul. God has given us the gift of grace by which we can live the virtues.

In the darkest days of the Second World War, Winston Churchill delivered a famous speech in which he referenced — not by name, but in essence — Thomas Aquinas on courage. Courage is the essential quality for the virtues. It takes courage to have faith; it takes courage to have hope; it takes courage to love; it takes courage to be prudent; it takes courage to act justly; it takes courage to practice temperance; and it takes courage to practice the virtue which itself is the manifestation of courage — fortitude. In that same war, during the Blitz, Queen Elizabeth, wife of King George VI, was asked if the two princesses were going to be evacuated.

She famously replied, "The children won't go without me. I won't leave without the king. And the king will never leave."

Wars among peoples come and go. We are always, however, engaged in a spiritual warfare between God and the prince of lies. And we have an Eternal King, Who is the source of all courage. Christ the King says to us, "Be of good cheer. I AM with you even to the end of the world" (see Matt. 28:20).

17

The Facts of Life

or

How Evil Drowns Out Truth with Sentimentality

Physical science can tell us only about the bare fact of things. The "why" of things comes from the God Who orders all facts. Believe in God, and you live the truth; deny God, and you have to come up with lies.

All that we are is because there is a God—a Three-in-One and One-in-Three. To deny that is to enter into the biggest lie of all: that life itself is an accident. If we don't understand that life is a gift, we will only be able to see death as a curse. We know the desultory grief of watching others die, and we know the anxiety of contemplating our own death. These can be overwhelming if we do not understand that death, through the rebirth of the soul, can be the entrance to eternal life. If people do not trust that God offers us eternal life, they will become obsessed with death and its anxiety. And then they will begin to turn that death of the self into a death imposed on others.

We can try to live a lie, but the truth of death cannot be denied. Indeed, every attempt to sanitize death creates a culture of lies. In turn, we leverage that culture of lies into a culture of death. The contraceptive mentality, the abortion mentality, and the euthanasia mentality can survive only on lies. *Roe v. Wade* was based on lies—lies about the Constitution, the right of privacy, the facts of biology, and life itself. In fact, the litigation that led to *Roe* was based on an admitted personal lie by the woman who was used to bring the case. This woman, Norma McCorvey, has since received the grace of Baptism, living a truth instead of a lie.

Many international organizations propagate the mentality of death by lying about population, by lying about the nature of laws and their potential to promote or to destroy life. The dire predictions from decades ago about population and the ability of civilization to handle more people were wrong. Pope Paul VI, in his encyclical *Humanae vitae*, laid down basic truths that go beyond the statistics and predictions of so-called experts. Those who did not want to accept these truths simply covered their ears. If you don't want to accept the truth, you have to smother it.

I remember standing next to an elderly Jewish woman at a pro-life meeting. During an opening prayer, a group of pro-abortion activists began to blow whistles in order to drown out the prayer. They could not contradict the fact that we were there; they could not contradict the fact that we were praying; and they could not contradict the fact of God. They could only try to cover it up by blowing whistles. The elderly Jewish woman turned to me and said, "I've heard that sound before. I grew up in Germany, and I can remember when the Nazis first started. They would send the Nazi Youth into the parks, and when anti-Fascist speakers mounted the podium and tried to be heard, the youth were instructed to blow whistles."

Elsewhere in the Second World War, Russian troops massacred hundreds upon hundreds of Polish officers in the Katyn Forest. The Russians claimed afterward that the Nazis had done it, but now we know the truth. We also know that the soldiers who machine-gunned the Polish officers and threw them into mass graves were given extra rations of vodka. In other words, they were cruel, but they were human. They had a conscience. If the conscience is going to condone death, it has to live a lie; and if it's going to live a lie, it has to anesthetize the truth.

Now, it is also easy to be so committed to the truth that one loses confidence in the ability of truth to survive on its own; we think and act as if it depends on us. The truth will always out in the end, but people committed to the truth can become so frustrated when they see lies against it that they lose their balance. This is how fanatics are created. Every righteous cause has had a fanatic (or several). There are fanatics in the pro-life movement just as there were fanatics in the abolitionist movement, such as John Brown, who attacked the federal arsenal at Harpers Ferry. I know a library in New York City that boasts a framed whisker from the beard of John Brown. But he was not a hero: He came close to destroying the progress of emancipation by his fanaticism. He lacked balance, but that does not deny the truth in which he believed.

When I was a college student, I remember going to the opera with my parents to see *Faust*. In the climactic scene, a woman in prison takes her baby and dashes it to the ground. We were close enough to see that the baby was, of course, a doll, but when that diva smashed the doll to the stage, my mother let out a scream! I was young and immature and naïve enough about life to be embarrassed by that maternal scream. Now I realize that in that maternal scream was the sense of truth that allowed me to be born and that has allowed, from all ages, every life to be born.

That holy scream was also heard in Bethlehem soon after Our Lord was born. An insecure willful king massacred the innocents because wanted to live a lie: He wanted to be the only king. But the lie did not last (no lie does), and he ended up dying a miserable death. In the meantime, many infants paid the price for his lie. Notice this characteristic of King Herod, which is typical of people like him: He was sentimental, and he played on sentimentality in others. When the three mysterious figures from the East told him that the Great One had been born, he responded, "Go and search diligently for the child, and when you have found him bring me word, that I too may come and worship him" (Matt. 2:8). We can almost see the saccharine look on his face, the pretense to devotion, while his mind was sneering and plotting.

Flannery O'Connor, the great Southern Catholic writer, pointed out many times that the cruelest people are the most sentimental. They don't live by truth, but by a lie. And when you live by a lie, you are governed, not by fact, but by feeling. Indeed, the worst crimes against life are always cloaked in sentimentality.

Here's a real fact—one you won't hear in many quarters because it is suppressed: Couples who practice the teaching of the Church by refusing contraception have a negligible divorce rate. Compare that with the divorce rate of some 50 percent among couples who practice contraception. This is a simple fact, but you will not hear it very often because it contradicts prevailing sentiment.

Here's another fact: The Holy Catholic Church is our Mother. In a culture of death, She not only preserves the spark of life but transmits that life to a dying culture. In the pope's cathedral, the Basilica of Saint John Lateran, a Latin inscription in the Baptistery says, as we might translate: "Here is born a people of divine lineage, generated by the Holy Spirit who makes these waters life-giving. Mother Church gives birth to her children within these waves."

18

The Divine Plan

or

How Trusting God's Providence
Is Essential to Flourishing

Either there is a plan for existence, or there isn't. All things proceed according to a divine design, or they are all essentially meaningless.

Our Lord is the Beginning and the End. He knows the past beyond our memory, and He foresees the future beyond our imagination. He tells us that all will be well with Him. This is not mere optimism or wishful thinking but is grounded in historical reality. When civilizations have denied providence, chaos has followed.

The Romans had a god of the New Year named Janus, from which we get the name of our first month. Janus had two faces that allowed him to look backward and forward. It was a graphic way of depicting the human adventure. But the True God is not two-faced. No one ever accused Jesus of duplicity. They accused Him of blasphemy and of being dangerously wrong about Himself, but they never accused Him of being two-faced. It was His honesty that made liars shrink from Him; it was His sense of purpose that inspired the good and bewildered the bad. The purposefulness of

God in creation requires that everything we do cooperate with His design.

And so the Church teaches us that even the simplest kind of work can be a majestic cooperation with providence. Pope John Paul II, in his encyclical *Laborem exercens*, on the dignity of labor, cautions us against thinking that work is a curse that we inherit because of the Fall of our disobedient ancestors. Adam and Eve did disobey, but work became a curse only because they began to lose a sense of its purpose. Everything we do can be consecrated—getting up in the morning, getting the family in order, doing the daily chores. Indeed, the simpler and more menial the task, when done in humility and love, becomes the greatest means of grace.

This vision of work extends to the Christian community gathered in the Church. The chief work of mankind is the worship of God, and so neither is this a curse. As work done as stewards of God's creation is not drudgery, neither should the worship of God be drudgery. But Our Lord knows why we're tempted to think that work and worship can be drudgery: We've been disappointed by too many people to trust easily that there is a divine plan for existence.

This is why it is hard to persuade men and women that God has a plan and that that plan is good: We have been pursued and attacked by Satan in the form of despair of God's goodness and providence. That's why St. Peter says so movingly, "Be sober, be watchful. Your adversary the devil prowls around like a roaring lion, seeking some one to devour. Resist him, firm in your faith" (1 Pet. 5:8–9). Peter had been morally bruised: He denied Our Lord, and he reeled in shock at what he had done. But it was humility—honesty about the human condition—that enabled him to go back to Our Lord. Our Lord humbles us, but He never humiliates us. We are the ones who humiliate ourselves when we act as though He has no plan for us.

In the Fall of man, our first ancestors bought into the lie that they were gods. Well, if we are gods, then we are in a pretty miserable state. We know (or should know) that we cannot control events for very long. The denial of God manifests itself in atheism, existentialism, materialism, utilitarianism — all those "isms" that are sicknesses from that first trauma. Our Lord came into the world, however, to heal it. He gave us Himself. This is what the Church is: When we say the Church is the Body of Christ, that means that She is the consoling and redeeming presence of Christ healing that trauma of denial, of deceit, of futility.

In 1987, in an address to the Roman Curia, Pope John Paul II spoke about the two personalities of the Church, both essential and both good: the Petrine and the Marian. The Petrine is the character of the Church as an authority. Christ is the Author of Life, and He passes on that life through the authority He gives to the Church. This authority is lived out in a special way in the sacrament of Marriage, by which He gives the gift of the bond of love, of procreation, and of mutual obedience. By cooperating with God in this sacrament, the man and the woman participate in the divine life-giving plan. After all, life and love are inseparable — and openness to life is the unconditional evidence of true love.

So, too, does the Petrine tradition of authority show through in the sacrament of Holy Orders, whereby deacons, priests, and bishops are given the ability and the duty to pass on the truth of God's plan. Further, in the sacrament of Reconciliation God gives the power to His priests to absolve sin. "If you forgive the sins of any, they are forgiven; if you retain the sins of any, they are retained" (John 20:23). And the sacrament of Anointing of the Sick is part of this authority of life and love — the gift of healing in the human order for the ultimate purpose of healing in the spiritual order, that we might be fit citizens for the Eternal Kingdom.

Complementing this Petrine personality of the Church is the Marian personality. As Peter is given authority, so Mary is given the grace of intercession. By her act of offering her will to the divine will, God's plan is carried through rebirth in Baptism, through the endowment of the gifts of the Holy Spirit in their fullness in Confirmation, and through the nurturing of the soul in the Holy Eucharist with Christ's own Body and Blood. Birth, formation of the soul, nourishment: These maternal gifts complement the Petrine gift of authority. The Petrine and the Marian personalities of the Church are given to the human race so that we might be faithful instruments of His gift of life and that we might further His purposes in the world.

The highest of all things we can do is to praise God for having given us the gift of life with which we participate in His plan. At the summit of all human activity is the worship of God. It's not meant to be at the end of everything we do, but at the start and in the heart of everything we do. That, in fact, is why the Church changed the Sabbath from the last day of the week to the first, for the Resurrection was on a Sunday, and so was the descent of the Holy Spirit upon the Church.

The Second Vatican Council, in its document *Optatam totius*, says that the entire Christian community is obliged to foster priestly vocations, and this we do by living our daily lives as Christians to the fullest. This simply means that God will provide ministers for His Church to the degree that Christians are Christians — doing our ordinary work, forming and nurturing families, and being witnesses to the gift of divine grace. When that happens, people see God's hand at work and respond to His call to serve Him as the servants of the people in Holy Orders.

Pope Benedict XVI wrote about a desert monk who had a vision of the devil.[9] The devil was ferociously ugly, just as expected, but

[9] *The Spirit of the Liturgy* (San Francisco: Ignatius Press, 2000), 193.

there was one strange thing about him that the monk reflected on afterward: Satan had no knees. The essence of Satan, therefore, is that he will not bow before God. He denies God's providence, and he wants us to do the same. He does not want us to kneel before the Lord, the Giver of all life. He wants us to disdain the seven sacraments. He wants us to pretend that the Eucharist is less than the presence of Christ Himself.

The first part of the Rite of the Eucharist in the Mass is the teaching part, the Pro-Anaphora. Here, the Church reminds us that God is God and that Satan is Satan. Timothy, one of the early teachers of the Church, in his second letter, having learned from St. Paul certainly, says:

> I charge you in the presence of God and of Christ Jesus who is to judge the living and the dead, and by his appearing and his kingdom: preach the word, be urgent in season and out of season, [reprove], rebuke, and exhort, be unfailing in patience and in teaching. For the time is coming when people will not endure sound teaching, but having itching ears they will accumulate for themselves teachers to suit their own likings, and will turn away from listening to the truth and wander into myths. (2 Tim. 4:1–4)

There are three verbs in this passage we should pay special attention to: "Reprove" means to guide and to bring back onto the straight way those who have gone astray. To reprove is an act of faith and trust in the providence of God. "Exhort" means to encourage; it is the obligation of each Christian to promote the pilgrimage of life according to God's design. This is the virtue of hope at work. "Rebuke" refers to tough love, warning us that we are always in this world on the edge of an abyss, and that abyss gets bigger and bigger the more people persuade a civilization that life is an accident. Love guides. Love rebukes. Love sets the example.

Grace and Truth

Our Lord does not so much tell us these things as He shows us them by leading us along the way. If there were no divine plan for life, we would not have any idea of progress; we would have no desire for scientific investigation; we would not want to exercise the imagination whatsoever. Our Lord encourages culture by walking through history, by walking through His own chosen land two thousand years ago, and by walking through our lives today.

Jesus told the Apostles in preparing the Last Supper that they would find all things as He told them, and so they found the Upper Room. If we live the life of grace, then, when our eyes close in death, they will open again in a larger world, and we will find all things just as He told us.

19

A Just War

or

How We Must Fight Evil for the Sake of Our Souls and Society

It seems a long time ago already, but the ushering in of the third millennium was accompanied by extravagant festivities around the world—chief of which was the Holy Year declared by the pope. But the secular celebrations, spectacular as they were, had a certain banality to them—not exactly a sense of exhaustion, but an inability, or an unwillingness, to do anything beyond what was merely entertaining. There were merry-go-rounds and fireworks and Ferris wheels, but very little in the way of great art or new, sumptuous symphonies. In London they built a Millennium Dome at enormous expense, but it soon became a white elephant. No one knew quite what to put in it. But most importantly, no one could find a place for God. No matter how we celebrate the passage of time, He remains the Lord of Eternity.

Amid the effervescence of those celebrations, there was a certain self-confidence, even smugness that a New Age had come into being in which human conflict had ended. What were we going to do with peace? How were we going to handle this overwhelm-ingly prosperous economy? How were we going to spend budget surpluses? One writer, Francis Fukuyama, even talked about "the end of history," by which he meant that everything really signifi-cant had been done, that liberal democracy was the final point of human political evolution, and now we could sit back and enjoy the fruits of our labors, as though the third millennium would be the Sabbath after mankind's working week.

Things changed very quickly. History will be over only when God decides to bring all things back into Himself. Wars are not over. As soon as the millennium began, we found our nation under attack. Not long ago now, we went to the moon. A generation later, how did we celebrate a new millennium? We didn't go to any place outside our orb; we literally went around in circles on Ferris wheels. Our sense of adventure was lost, and a certain naïveté set in.

The shock of reality has awakened us to the fact that we are always engaged in some kind of war. The twentieth century saw over six hundred official wars, and we don't know how many there will be in the future. The Church has pondered the human fact of warfare in greater depth than any other institution. There are some who would equate Christianity with pacifism, but pacifism has as much to do with peace as Puritanism has to do with purity.

St. Augustine said that there are seven standards by which we can justify going into battle, known as *jus ad bellum*:

- *Just cause*: War must be in response to a direct and unjust attack upon the just order of life and freedom.
- *Proper authority*: War must be declared and prosecuted by a legitimate government, entrusted by the people to decide whether or not the cause is just.
- *Right intention*: The intention in going to war cannot be revenge, but must involve correcting a wrong, preventing a miscarriage of justice, protecting life, and so on.

- *Proportionality:* The just war must be fought in such a way that no more evil results than the good that results. That's a very hard thing to guarantee, but at least there must be an intention to promote the good and not to compound evil.

- *Reasonable chance of success:* A just war cannot be a suicidal adventure, a manifestation of mere bravado. Remember the story of the charge of Light Brigade, when British troops in the Crimean War went on a suicidal charge against an overwhelming enemy. A French officer who watched the scene said, "It is magnificent, but it is not war."

- *Last resort:* All other attempts at peace must have been explored; all discussion must be exhausted.

- *Peace:* The just war must end in peace. That, again, is hard to guarantee, but the intention of establishing peace must prevail over the desire simply to create a situation in which another war is inevitable.

It's very hard to talk about war from one's armchair. Those most qualified to talk about war are those who have fought in them, and the greatest of those men tend to be the least ready to discuss what they've seen. They know the horror of it; they know it's not a game. Who is a more colorful, courageous, and successful soldier than the great Duke of Wellington, victor of the Battle of Waterloo? He said that next to a battle lost, there is nothing more tragic than a battle won—for even in victory good men die. It is the general who sees that firsthand, who walks through the fields and sees the dying and the dead, who bears on his conscience the responsibility for that carnage.

St. Augustine tells us that in addition to standards for going to war, there are also standards for the conduct of the war, known as *jus in bello.* Now, St. Augustine did not speak as an armchair observer.

He lived in North Africa in the fourth and fifth centuries, which was a field of constant turmoil. He watched the Roman Empire falling down around him. But he also wrote about the contrast between the city of man and the city of God: He knew that even if we win an earthly battle, there is still a heavenly battle to be fought.

St. Augustine's principles of *jus in bello* can be split into two categories. First, the force we use must not be out of proportion to the end desired. That is, we shouldn't cause more destruction to attain victory than is necessary. Second, in any just war, every effort must be made to protect the innocent from harm. As we look at Augustine's diocese in Hippo, we see desolation now: It is not a Christian place anymore. Where there were dozens and dozens of dioceses, now the Church is just a symbolic remnant. Wars have been fought there, and the cross has been removed.

Christian history includes a great deal of violence done by man against the Church. There have been times when popes themselves have gone to war to protect Christian civilization. In the sixteenth century, Pope Pius V organized a league of the Papal States, the Venetian Republic, Spain, and the Holy Roman Empire to fight the threat of the Ottoman Turks. This culminated in what was the largest naval battle in history until the Second World War, fought off the coast of Greece. As the battle raged, the pope had his top officials pray the Rosary. It took weeks for news of the battle to reach Rome, but at a certain point during the recitation of the Rosary, the Holy Father stopped. He looked out the window and, while the Mediterranean Sea was hundreds of miles away, he saw the battle; he could describe it; it was vivid to him. And he told his advisors to sing a Te Deum, because a great victory had been won. At that very hour, it was indeed so.

A century later, in 1683, the Polish king John III Sobieski confronted Ottoman troops outside the gates of Vienna. The victory he won, in the name of the Faith, saved Christian Europe. The

English writer Hilaire Belloc said that that date should be engraved in every civilized mind for what it meant for Christian civilization. That date was, perhaps coincidentally, September 11.

And so there will always be war. But even if there were some kind of halcyon time in which all arms were laid down, there would still be a deeper warfare.

Our Lord said that He could see warfare in Heaven (see Rev. 12). That warfare against God, that enmity of pride against the Lord of Life, seeped into this world as soon as it was made. Our first ancestors struggled in that battle, and they lost. And so sin and death themselves infected the world—but they do not define this world. There have been Christian heretics who thought that the world from its first moment was intrinsically evil, but God said it was good—and God does not deceive us. That is precisely why we must fight to preserve the good in our earthly struggle against sin and death.

Our civilization is engaged in a deep, spiritual war for the dignity of life itself that manifests itself outwardly in political and legal confrontation. We can take those standards of warfare that St. Augustine gave us and apply them to the crusade to protect life in the womb. This is the most just of wars. What could be a more just cause than the protection of the most innocent life at its very beginning? And who has a better authority to protect life than the mother, the father, and the government, which is ordained to protect the right to life and liberty and the pursuit of happiness? In all these ways, God is testing the courage of our society, because we have not only the privilege but the duty to defend life. In fact, St. Thomas Aquinas tells us that it can even be a sin not to defend life for a just cause.

In a cause so noble as fighting for the right to life, there are, of course, some extravagant and unfettered people who violate the standards of a just war, such as those who resort to violence in the protection of the unborn. These fanatical people destroy the cause that they would defend by their lack of mental and moral discipline. A fanatic, it has been said, is somebody who thinks that God would agree with him if God had all the facts. The right to life will be secure because of people who, quietly praying and using the supernatural weaponry of grace, will overcome evil. Our Lord says that in a spiritual battle, there are some things that can be cast out only by fasting and prayer. The right to life, that is, cannot be defended with a gun.

There is another battle that is being fought in our generation for the soul of the Church. There are some who would reduce the Church to a mere institution, a kind of rubber stamp for prevailing cultural attitudes, rather than seeing Her as the Mystical Body of Christ. This, again, is a warfare that can be resolved only by fasting and by prayer. But the violence against Heaven and earth cannot be underestimated.

I have a crucifix that stirs the virtue of piety—not the virtue of religion as piety, but piety in the classical sense of reverence for one's ancestors. My father once found a crucifix lying in a trash heap outside, I am sorry to say, a convent. He rescued the figure of Christ, the corpus. He was like Joseph of Arimathea, finding a repository for the body of Christ. The crucifix he made, which I have, is finer than the original one. Now, my father did not speak openly very much about his faith, but this was his way of engaging in the battle for the soul of the Church.

He did not notice me one night going by his workbench when was putting the corpus on the new cross he had built. While he nailed Christ to the cross, he had put a handkerchief over the figure. That was a subtle victory for the Lord being fought by my father. There was an exquisite piety, as a religious virtue, expressed there. We often speak so easily and even blithely about the Crucifixion, but my father could not bear even to drive tacks into a clay figure of Our Lord.

A Just War

Each one of us is engaged in this spiritual warfare, and each one of us is being tested each day. There is no cause more just than that of Christ. And if we fight this spiritual warfare by fasting, by prayer, by joyfully living our daily routine according to the life of the virtues, then, by God's grace, we will hear the voice of Christ saying to us, "Well done, good and faithful servant; ... enter into the joy of your master" (Matt. 25:23).

20

Mothers and Children

or

How the Grace and Truth of Christ Is Passed Down

There was a moment when Our Lord raised His hands and eyes in prayer: "I thank thee, Father, Lord of heaven and earth, that thou hast hidden these things from the wise and understanding and revealed them to babes" (Matt. 11:25). There are certain things that the learned and clever have a hard time understanding. They are good at reasoning things out, but faced with something more glorious than our limited reason can comprehend, the learned and the clever are at a loss.

Little children, on the other hand, take glory for granted. A small child is not surprised by an ocean any more than he's surprised by a drop of water: They're both new to him. And a small child is not perplexed by a volcano any more than by a lighted match: Both of them are alluring and threatening to him. Our Lord says, "Unless you turn and become like children, you will never enter the kingdom of heaven" (Matt. 18:3). Without that childlike openness to possibilities beyond our human reason, Heaven itself becomes an impossibility—and the glory of Heaven becomes positively horrible. Innocence is the love of Heaven, and thus the gateway to the glory of Heaven.

The preternatural intelligence of Adam and Eve enabled them to rejoice in the glory of God *with the use of reason* in the same way that children rejoice in the glory of God *by a lack of reason*. All that has changed. The human race, having lost Paradise, embarked upon a struggle to contemplate and make sense of the world God had entrusted to it.

The twentieth century is an especially glaring and glorious image of the failures and successes of the human race in dealing with the glory of God and the tragedy of sin. We are accountable for what we learn from that experience. Those who lived through much of that century are said to have belonged to "the greatest generation." They endured two world wars and a historic Depression. They saw the greatest advance of human science the world has ever seen. People in that generation were born when horses were still used for transportation, and they lived to see a man walking on the moon. The greatest generation enlisted the virtues and put them into a glorious combat against lies and for truth, against iniquity and for justice. And they lived through that century taking on wound after wound; they died bearing the scars of that human drama.

God can do what He wants with this world. He didn't have to come to us; He did and does so gratuitously. He could have come into this world any way He wanted, but He chose to be born of a mother. And He tells us that we will inherit, by His grace, a New Mother, the Heavenly Jerusalem. Every great generation is made great by that vision, by the promise of eternal glory. Banality breeds banality; sin breeds sin. But glory grows from one glory to another, and virtue builds upon virtue.

These virtues and vices can be passed from one generation to the next. Great generations, therefore, need great mothers. Our Lord offers each one of us that greatness by offering each one of us the same Mother — His own Mother. When Our Lord hung on the Cross, after having prayed for the forgiveness of those who were killing Him, and after promising Paradise to the thief on His side, He looked down from the Cross and said to John, "Behold your mother" (John 19:27).

I remember looking at a painting of the Crucifixion with my mother. I played the part of the art historian by explaining the artist, the biography of the artist, why he is considered a master painter, what techniques he used, and so on. That's how I explained the Crucifixion scene, with our Lord on the Cross and His Mother weeping. But when I finished, my mother simply said, "How difficult it must have been for her." I got the painting right; she got the Mother right. That intuitive gift of the mother is passed down to each generation through the Church, Our Holy Mother. The gift of motherhood must never be taken for granted.

Every mother is a prophet of life. When a civilization abandons its children, it is the mother who reminds us of the desolation. We call the university an *Alma Mater* because it is an institution that passes on the tradition of culture. Because universities have lost their heart for being guardians of culture, they've even forgotten how to translate those simple Latin words. The motherly teacher passing on the lore of the tribe reminds the world of the eternal contest between life and death.

My mother was gentle, but she could be severe when anyone criticized one of four people: the pope, the queen (her parents were English), the cardinal who received her and my father into the Church, and Mother Teresa. My mother met Mother Teresa at one of her convents, and they spoke to each other as though they had known each other for a lifetime, like two ladies chatting over the back fence. After all, they were both mothers: My mother was a mother of a family, and Mother Teresa was a mother of many families.

Grace and Truth

When my mother was dying, she became unconscious. At one point, I began singing some hymns to her, thinking that they might register. She showed no sign of understanding what I was saying. Then I prayed to Mother Teresa: "Mother, please help my mother." As I said that, my mother briefly became conscious, looked at me, and said, "Love."

Love gives life. At the beginning of creation, the Holy Spirit breathed upon the face of the waters, the womb of the universe. And whatever language the Holy Spirit spoke, He said, "Love," and all things came into being. In the fullness of time, when Our Lady said that she would cooperate with God's will, the Holy Spirit overshadowed her, and in whatever language He speaks, He said, "Love," and Love Himself was conceived within Her body. Love opens the veil between time and eternity, between earth and Heaven. It was Love crying on the Cross that split the veil of the temple in Jerusalem.

In the Second Book of Maccabees, Judas Maccabeus is recorded as saying that it is good to pray for the dead, and so he prayed for his fellow dead. It is the earliest record we have of gratuitous love interceding for those who have gone on before. The veil between Heaven and earth is much thinner than we believe—and when the dead go to Our Lord in a state of grace, they can be closer to us than they ever were on earth.

When I was a child, we didn't gather around the television or the computer screen, but around the piano, and we sang old songs. (That's how I got my repertory of nineteenth-century ballroom songs.) One of my mother's favorite songs was about a grandfather's clock, and it included the line, "It was bought on the morn of the day he was born and was always his pleasure and pride. / But it stopped short, never to go again, when the old man died. Tick tock, tick tock." My mother died at twenty minutes after one on a Sunday morning. When I got home, the house was empty, and the clock was stopped at twenty minutes after one. It would be childish to make too much of that—but if we're really childlike, we will simply take the divine coincidence for granted. Remember how Our Lord prayed, "I thank thee, Father, Lord of heaven and earth, that thou hast hidden these things from the wise and understanding and revealed them to babes."

One of the greatest minds that has ever lived, John Henry Cardinal Newman, understood the meaning and mystery of truth. That is why for his memorial inscription he chose *Ex umbris et imaginibus in veritatem*, "Out of the shadows and imagining, into the truth." "Into the truth," not around the truth, or near the truth, or behind the truth. Our limited intellects are clever and learned enough to do that. But he wanted to go *into the truth*.

Christ is the Truth. When He rose from the dead, He stood on the shore of the Sea of Galilee and called out to His men in the boat. These were strong grown men, hauling in their nets, going back to the only thing they really knew how to do, trying to figure out what this death and Resurrection meant. But Christ called out, "Children, have you any fish?" (John 21:5). That is the Voice of Eternity. And those men, I am certain, when they heard themselves called children by Christ, thought they were in Heaven.

About the Author

Father George Rutler has long been a pastor of parishes in the heart of New York City. He holds numerous academic degrees from the United States and Europe and is the author of thirty books. He has broadcast programs on EWTN since the early 1980s.

GRACE
&
TRUTH

TWENTY STEPS TO
EMBRACING VIRTUE AND
SAVING CIVILIZATION

FR. GEORGE RUTLER